TAMING *Lil' Mo*

THE "TELL-ALL" BOOK FROM
CYNTHIA LOVING

NEXT LEVEL PUBLISHING

Next Level Publishing
PO Box 83
Newark, NJ 07101

If you purchase this book without a cover you should be aware that this book may have been stolen property and reported as "unsold and destroyed" to the publisher. In such case neither the author nor the publisher has received any payment for this "stripped book."

Taming Lil' Mo

Copyright © 2014 by Cynthia Loving c/o Next Level Publishing

All rights reserved, including the right to reproduce this book or portions thereof in any form whatsoever.

ISBN (10)   0-9-80015472
ISBN (13):   978-0980015478

Manufactured in the United States of America

Cover Photo By: JaTawny Chatmon (JatawnyMChatmon.com)
Hair: Charese TheArtist Adkins
Makeup: Kash (KashBarbBookings@gmail.com)
Stylist: Orlando (DaArtist15@gmail.com)

Cover Layout & Design: HotBookCovers.com
Editing: Michele Barard

For more info and copies email: info@nextlevelpublishing.com or visit www.nextlevelpublishing.com

For You

I sincerely want to dedicate this to YOU. Yes, YOU reading this right at this moment. I am humbly honored that you found something in me attractive, that you invested your time to read about my testimony. Thank You for believing in me. You give me life. So I owe you these words of dedication to show my sincerest appreciation. XoXo…

- Cynthia p/k/a Lil' Mo

Gracias

Thank You GOD for giving me the strength to finally share my TESTIMONY. I love YOU for trusting me to share my ministry.

To my Husband Karl Sharif Dargan. You are everything to me, I absolutely adore you. My children: Heaven, God'Iss-Love, Khamir, Justin, Iendia, Kiley, and Jonah. Nothing else exists outside of our world. Momma Diddy and Diddy I love you more than you can phathom. Charese, Norman, Brey'N, Brey'Cyn, Brey'Ent, and CeAnna… my brothers James and Tim. I love YOU ALL so much.

My mom Carla, Jerraya, Jaz, Sharp and your beautiful family, Pop, Jeff, Nijah and all NORTH PHILLY FAMILY and Baltimore family. All my Family (related and real friends in real life) the list is short of those I claim.

The whole Next Level Publishing family for making this dream of mine come true. Dashawn Taylor and Aleasha Arthur you are amazing. Thank you for bringing my vision to LIFE.

My HoneyChild Entertainment Inc team and my management and consultant team for going on this revealing journey with me. To all that have come and gone in and out of my life, I have learned so much from MY mistakes, my past, my shortcomings and my failures. I can't say that I've had the perfect life like I once portrayed. I am going to let the battle within continue. Neither one of ME wins. I just continue to fight to be great. I finally have made peace with my past. I LOVE ME!

Lil' Mo Discography

5 Minutes	Lil' Mo feat. Missy Elliot
Ta Da	Lil' Mo
Superwoman Pt. II	Lil' Mo feat Fabolous
Gangsta	Lil' Mo
4Ever	Lil' Mo
Ten Commandments	Lil' Mo feat. Lil' Kim
Hot Boys, Hot Girls	Lil' Mo feat. Lil' Wayne
Sumtimes	Lil' Mo feat. Jim Jones
Lucky Her	Lil' Mo
I Love Me	Lil' Mo feat. Tweet
Take Me Away	Lil' Mo feat. Maino
I'm A Diva	Lil' Mo
L's Up	Lil' Mo
Hot Boyz	Missy Elliot feat. Lil' Mo
Wifey	Next feat Lil' Mo
Whatever	Idea feat. Lil' Mo
I'll Trade (A Million Bucks)	Keith Sweat feat. Lil' Mo
Put It On Me	Ja Rule feat. Lil' Mo & Vita
I Cry	Ja Rule feat. Lil' Mo
Lay It Down	Jermaine Dupri & R.O.C. feat. Lil' Mo
Pray For Me	Mobb Deep feat. Lil' Mo
Where's My...?	Adam F feat. Lil' Mo
If I Could Go	Angie Martinez feat. Lil' Mo & Sacario
Can't Let You Go	Fabolous feat. Lil' Mo & Mike Shorey
Thick & Thin	E-40 feat. Lil' Mo
Endow Me	Coko feat. Lil' Mo, Fantasia & Faith Evans
Bulletproof Love	Foxy Brown feat. Lil' Mo
Cry	LL Cool J feat. Lil' Mo
It Ain't Love	MSTRKRFT feat. Lil' Mo
21 Answers	Lil' Mo feat. Free
Yeah Yeah Yeah	Lil' Mo feat. Miri Ben-Ari
Do You Wanna Ride	Yo Yo, Kelly Price, Missy Elliot & Lil' Mo
It's Alright	Queen Latifah, Faith Evans & Lil' Mo
Mr. D.J.	Missy Elliot, Lady Saw & Lil Mo
Good Morning Heartache	Ol' Dirty Bastard feat. Lil' Mo
Is This The End	3rd Storee & Lil' Mo
Girlfriend/Boyfriend	Blackstreet, Janet Jackson, Ja Rule, Eve & Lil' Mo

Tell Me	Case, Levar A. Wilson & Lil' Mo
Hello It's Me	Gerald LeVert & Lil' Mo
Parking Lot Pimpin	Jay-Z, Memphis Bleek, Beanie Sigel & Lil' Mo
Somebody's Gonna Die Tonight	Dave Bing feat. Lil' Mo
That's What I'm Looking For	Da Brat, Jermaine Durpi, Missy Elliot & Lil' Mo
Club 2G	Missy Elliot & Lil' Mo
Bounce With Me	Lil Bow Wow, R.O.C. & Lil' Mo
Last Night	Changing Faces & Lil' Mo
Monica	Before Dark & Lil' Mo
Straight Up	Chante Moore & Lil' Mo
No Direspect	Tamar Braxton, Missy Elliot & Lil' Mo
Shotgun	Torrey Carter & Lil' Mo
Keep It G.A.N.G.S.T.A.	Nate Dogg, Xzibit & Lil' Mo
Interlude	DJ Clue & Lil' Mo
Hi Maintenance	Yukmouth & Lil' Mo
Take You Home	Fabolous & Lil' Mo
Can't Deny It	Fabolous, Nate Dogg & Lil' Mo
Niggaz Nature (Remix)	2Pac & Lil' Mo
Wrong Idea	Bad Azz & Lil' Mo
No Playaz	Angie Martinez, Tony Sunshine & Lil' Mo
Sponsor	Canela Cox & Lil' Mo
All Those Fancy Things	Koffee Brown & Lil' Mo
Wore Out Your Welcome	Allure & Lil' Mo
So Low	Tha Eastsidaz & Lil' Mo
Finders Keepers	Jaheim & Lil' Mo
I've Changed	Missy Elliot & Lil' Mo
I Know Whutchu Like	Mocha, Petey Pablo, Missy Elliot & Lil' Mo
Mardi Gras	Mocha, Missy Elliot & Lil' Mo
The Streetz	Mocha & Lil' Mo
Daddy Get the Cash	Styles P. & Lil' Mo
I've Come Too Far	Tina Moore & Lil' Mo
Ten Years	Darius Rucker & Lil' Mo
Why You Tell Me That	Ms. Jade & Lil' Mo
She Wanna Know	Joe Budden & Lil' Mo
Thug Nature	Sheek Louch & Lil' Mo
We Fly	Ja Rule, Vita, DJ Envy & Lil' Mo
Keep It Real	Nate Dogg, Fabolous & Lil' Mo
Holla At Somebody Real	Fabolous & Lil' Mo
Don't Stop The Music	E-40, Lil' Flip, DJ Kay Slay & Lil' Mo

Shake That Ass	Mannie Fresh & Lil' Mo
Freak Wit Me	Mannie Fresh & Lil' Mo
Chocolate Cities	Lady Luck & Lil' Mo
Never Stop Thuggin'	Knoc-turn'al & Lil' Mo
Hold Your Head Up High	Miri Ben-Ari & Lil' Mo
Solid Chic	Birdman & Lil' Mo
Could It Be	Snook da Rokk Star & Lil' Mo
Baby (Remix)	Fabolous & Lil' Mo
What Should I Do	Fabolous & Lil' Mo
Unbelievable	Whuteva & Lil' Mo
We Takin' Over	Remy Ma, Jacki-O, Trina, DJ Lazy K & Lil' Mo
Make Me Better (Remix)	Fabolous & Lil' Mo
Good Lovin'	Da Brat, DJ Cocoa, Chanelle & Lil' Mo
Lovely	Felicia "Snoop" Pearson & Lil' Mo
Nothing To Lose	Mancini & Lil' Mo
Prayer Song For Haiti	Kim Burrell, Musiq Soulchild, Tye Tribbett, James Hall, Nancey Jackson-Johnson, Michelle Williams, Nikki Ross, Anaysha Figueroa & Lil' Mo
Troubled World (Part 2)	Faith Evans, Estelle & Lil' Mo
U & Me	Ja Rule & Lil' Mo
Cut U Off	Trina & Lil' Mo

PART I

Based on a True Story

Prologue

"*P*lease, Jesus, don't let me die like this..."

I could barely get the prayer out of my mouth. Heavy blood leaked from the top of my head and nearly covered my entire face. There was total chaos in the back of the limousine. Never in my short life had I come so close to death. My ears were ringing like a church bell and I could barely focus my eyes. Screams echoed off the plush interior of the vehicle. I struggled to stay conscious. All I could see was red. My team was panicking and crying in the back of the limo as it tore down the highway en route to the hospital. I whispered another short prayer to the heavens. Thoughts of my family flashed in and out of my mind.

"Please, Jesus, don't let me die tonight..."

A few minutes earlier, I was leaving a sold out concert at The Warfield Theater. I had just wrapped up a promotional show for my new album. I was on a natural high and was preparing to jet to another city. As my team and I headed to the limousine we noticed a small crowd gathering near the vehicles. I heard a male voice scream my name.

"Lil' Mo!"

I turned around with a smile on my face. I looked up

expecting to see another fan reaching out for a hand shake, a quick picture, or maybe an autograph. I was sadly mistaken. There was no love waiting for me. Standing in front of me was a burly assailant with malice in his heart and the devil in his eyes. Before I could say a word to him, he yelled at me.

"Bitch!"

The harsh insult was quickly followed by what felt like a sledgehammer. The attacker mercilessly smashed me in the head with a heavy champagne bottle. The glass shattered and so did my face. I crumbled to the ground in a heap. My heel broke and I screamed. Hands shaking, I instinctively fumbled with my broken shoe. I didn't realize the severity of my injury until the blood flooded my clothes like a rainstorm. It was bad.

"Oh my God," one of my dancers screamed.

Hands frantically picked me up and tossed me in the back seat of the limo. My team tried to stop the bleeding but the white towels quickly turned burgundy red. Things were becoming serious. I kept sending prayers to my Lord and Savior Jesus Christ fearing that I would never see the light of day again. My career was just getting off the ground. My debut album was set to be released in just seventy two hours. *Who could have done this to me? What soul could be so dark?* I thought.

There was so much that I wanted to see and so much I wanted to do. I hadn't even started a family yet and it seemed that someone was trying to clip my wings for good. I thought about how unfair life was. I had worked so hard to get to that moment in my career and now I could lose it all in the blink of an eye. I said one more prayer and then started to accept my fate.

"Lord, this is not how I planned my life. But if this is the way I have to go out then Lord let your will be done. But, please, give me a chance to get my mommy and my daddy on the phone so I can say goodbye."

With those words, I felt a peace come over me. I never got a chance to make that call. It was nothing short of a miracle that I survived the assault. It seemed that God didn't want me to say goodbye that evening. He had a bigger plan for me. When you are blessed and highly favored, it seems the devil doesn't want to see you win. That horrific night was not the end of Lil' Mo. I was just getting started.

*

Chapter One

My mother screamed as loud as she could to the heavens. God and every blessed angel undoubtedly cringed at her cries for mercy. All the nurses started to scramble as the mood in the delivery room suddenly turned to a scene of panic. What was supposed to be a routine birth procedure quickly turned dangerous. My mother roared again in pain. It seemed like everyone in South Side Hospital knew something was wrong.

"Push, Cynthia!"

My father nervously raised his voice and squeezed his wife's hand. A mix of emotions consumed my daddy's heart. The excitement of witnessing the birth of his first child was replaced by the fear of his worst nightmare coming true. He had heard all the horror stories about countless women who died during child birth. My daddy tried his best to keep his composure but inside he was boiling over with fear. He said a silent prayer and asked God to see his wife through this excruciating struggle.

Another harsh pain hit my mother and she yelled

again. Her loud screams scared my daddy. An uneasy expression covered his young face. He quickly looked at the hospital staff. As fate would have it, my stubbornness and my enormous, hard head were making things complicated. Even after thirty-eight hours in labor, my mother still couldn't push me into this world. One of the doctors sensed that my life was in peril before I even tasted my first breath and ordered an emergency Cesarean.

"Honey, I'm right here," my daddy said to my mother. "It's goin' to be okay, Cindy."

My daddy tried to keep his voice calm despite the drama in the delivery room. He could see my mother was scared out of her mind. He continued to calm her and squeezed her hands tightly. My daddy needed my mother to know that he would be right by her side no matter what happened in that hospital.

The emergency procedure was a success. At exactly 11:49 p.m. on November 19th, I opened my eyes for the very first time. After nine months of total darkness I was greeted by the most beautiful ray of sunshine, my mother's smile. She greeted me with tears of joy and exhaustion. Despite all my crying, whining, and hollering, my parents gazed at me like I was the most amazing thing on earth.

My daddy's face gleamed with pride and excitement when he laid eyes on me. He held me carefully in his protective arms and looked at my mother. I could see the love deep in his eyes as my mom and dad shared a moment of deep connection. The bond between them was deeper than simply the attraction between a man and a woman. My parents were soul mates in every sense of the phrase. Their love had journeyed well beyond the mental and the physical and it was now entering the spiritual realm. I was only a few hours old but their feelings for each other had already consumed me. My first impression of life was that of love and family. Little did I know at the time, but those precious minutes that my parents shared in front of me would affect me deeply for many years to come.

For the first few hours of my life I was nameless. My parents wanted to wait until I was born to decide on what to call me. With my mother recovering from surgery, my father decided to give me the dearest name to his heart, Cynthia Karen Loving, Jr. the same name as my mother.

It's no mistake that I was born into the *Loving* family….literally. I was conceived by a West Virginia pretty-boy who crossed paths with a feisty young intellectual from the South Bronx. A chance meeting between two opposite personalities turned into young love and then exploded into a union that still exists today. Even as they approach forty years of marriage, their love is as strong as ever. I witnessed firsthand what love can do for a person and what it can do for a family. For as long as I could remember, my daddy taught me that having the last name *Loving* came with a sense of pride and responsibility.

"Kiddo, the most important thing in life is family first. We're a team. Never allow nothing to come in between the team. So whatever it takes, no matter how hard things get, it's always about the team. It's always about the family. Never forget that. It's family first."

My dad's words have stuck with me my entire life. I remember the conviction in his voice as he told me the true value of being a *Loving*.

"Always hold your name to the highest standards.

What goes on in private is nobody's business. You may be hurting and your family may have troubles, but never disrespect the family name. And when you are representing the *Loving* name you make sure you are representing it well."

For the past decade and a half the world has known me as Lil' Mo. My entertainment career has taken me around the globe countless times. I have recorded hit records and have performed with dozens of superstar acts. I have appeared in music videos, movies, and reality television shows. Millions of fans have fallen in love with Lil' Mo and have followed my journey as I battled through the trials and tribulations of this ruthless industry. Still, there's a secret that most people have never been privy to. When the music stops and the lights go down, something real happens. Lil' Mo dies.

She doesn't die in a literal sense, but she has to be removed. The minute I leave the stage and not long after the cameras stop rolling, I have to take Lil' Mo off like a heavy costume. I peel back the onion and feel just as naked as the day I came out of my mother. It's in that moment that Cynthia Karen Loving, Jr. is reborn.

For years, I purposely hid that side of me from the public's eye. I felt like I needed to keep that side of me locked away. Cynthia is the side of me that hurts and bleeds; that cries and mourns. More importantly, Cynthia is the side of me that loves.

It's been a long time since I heard her voice. I was afraid to let people know that side of me. The moment has finally come to introduce Cynthia to the world. I was once told that my life was too neat and that there was no dirt on me and my family. From growing up in the church and being raised by two loving parents, people on the outside have been probing my life and they swear that I'm as clean as a baby's police record. They see my family on television and in the magazines and they believe that I lived this perfect life.

The truth is stranger than fiction. I have not been able to tell the dark side of the Christian girl's story. I'm tired of tripping over the mountain of dirt that has been swept under the rug over the years. For a long time I was able to hide behind the fame and keep a protective smile on my face. Running from my past was never the right answer. You can't outrun your own demons. My story will be revealing. It may hurt a lot of people who carried a false perception of my life. It's like I have to pull off an old Band-Aid to reveal my ugly battle scars. It will hurt like hell, but it will also heal. I thank God for the courage to finally tell my story.

*

Chapter Two

The 1980s were a dangerous time in New York. The streets were filled with lost souls chasing that next high, that next trick, and that next dollar. Robberies, shootings and murders were common. The crime rate in the city was skyrocketing higher than the twin towers. Broken-down projects were infested with drug dealers hell-bent on serving fiends and protecting their territory. The streets were a war zone. In a few short years, the crack epidemic had destroyed lives and crippled communities throughout the five boroughs. Luckily, as a young child I was not exposed to that reality.

My neighborhood was a world away from the chaos in New York City. One of the first towns I grew up in was Medford, New York. My neighborhood was the typical Long Island community. The roads were lined with large homes and beautifully manicured lawns. By today's standards, you would think mini mansions surrounded my house. I grew up in a time when middle class was almost considered rich. The big homes in my area belonged to doctors, lawyers and working class types. We were the only black family in my neighborhood in Medford. One Hispanic family lived across the street but the rest of my neighbors were white. There were so many white families in my neighborhood that I used to think that I was white. You couldn't tell me otherwise.

Because we were the only blacks in our neighborhood people treated us differently. Some people were visibly bothered by our presence but most people treated us fairly. There were no burning crosses on our lawn or no racist graffiti on our house, but a number of racist incidents happened to me and my siblings while we were growing up in Medford. Despite the racial tension, my parents tried their best to protect us from it.

My mother was a schoolteacher on Long Island. My father worked odd jobs. He did everything from cab driving to photography. I'm not sure how we survived, but they worked hard to make sure we were well taken care of. My parents never wanted to raise us in a poor neighborhood. They hustled tirelessly to make sure we lived in a safe area. When it came to their kids, my parents were loving but also very protective and strict.

Before they had children my parents lived two totally different lives. My mother was a stickler for knowledge and heavy into the books. My father was simply off the chain. Before he met my mother, my daddy was wild and crazy. In fact, his nickname was "Wild Baby." The youngest of six kids my daddy was best known for being the preacher's son who stayed in trouble. Everyone who knew my father could never understand why he was such a problem child.

My daddy was raised in the church. His father was Reverend Richard M. Loving of Hope Missionary Baptist

Church. If you were involved in the civil rights movement in the 1950s and 1960s or if you were connected with any black churches in Long Island, you probably worked with Reverend Loving.

My grandfather was a heavy influence on the community. He fought for human rights and touched a lot of souls in Central Islip. People loved my grandfather. Many Long Island residents struggled and fought with him to make New York a better place for blacks and other minorities to live. The city of Central Islip eventually recognized my grandfather's remarkable impact on the community and named a street after him. He was truly a man for the people.

Despite all the accolades and success that my grandfather had, Reverend Loving could not get a hold on his youngest son, Wild Baby. As a young child, my dad would give his parents fits. He was always fighting and never hesitated to cause havoc around the city. Everyone knew he was Reverend Loving's son, but that didn't stop my father. He carried his rebellious nature into his teens and started running the streets. My family and everyone else who knew my dad was convinced that he would be wild and reckless forever.

But God had a different plan for my daddy. Most of us believe that we are in control of our own destiny. Then God throws us a curveball that changes everything. That curveball hit my daddy one day when he least expected it.

In the early 1970s in Long Island, young blacks were out and about expressing themselves like never before. Afros, bell-bottom pants, and soul music ruled the day. My daddy was always in the mix. The streets were like his second home. My daddy was always down to have some fun. A few of his friends and he decided to visit Dowling College for a party. Knowing my daddy, I'm sure he was trying to meet some unsuspecting young woman for a quick hookup, but before he could be introduced to the other woman, my daddy locked eyes with a smart young firecracker from the South Bronx. Her name was Cynthia Karen Miles.

My mother was a fighter who never backed down from anyone. From the moment she grabbed my father's attention, my mother made him totally forget all other women. Even after all of this time my father has never turned his eyes away from her.

That night at Dowling College changed my parent's lives. It didn't take long before they became an inseparable couple. They helped each other get their priorities in order and created an unbreakable bond. My mother's love consumed my father in a way that he had never felt before. The "Wild Baby" was now a changed man and the world was introduced to Jacob D. and Cynthia K. Loving.

A few years after they were married, my parents were blessed with four children, my brother, Tim, my sister, Charese, my youngest brother, James, and me. We are all very close in age. We are what people like to call back to back kids; you know when a woman has a baby and then goes for her six week checkup, or a little bit after that she finds out she's pregnant again? That's how we are. Only a few years separate the oldest and youngest of us. I guess my parents were busy back then.

Our family was tight when we were growing up. My parent always expressed their love in the house. They hugged and kissed in front of us naturally. My father complimented my mother a lot and told her how she pretty she was. Not only were my parents very affectionate towards each other but they were constantly preaching love and respect in our house. They wanted us to know that they loved each other and us very much. Their feelings spread throughout the household and we were truly a Loving Family.

My parents kept a very short leash on us kids. We were not allowed to spend time at other people's houses and we were never allowed to spend the night out unless it was with our family. If our friends wanted to come over, my parents would have to feel comfortable with them and also with their family. My mother and father didn't want anything to happen to their children. I guess that's why our household was so much fun. Between family day and crazy made-up games, my parents never missed an opportunity to entertain us and put a smile on our faces.

Have you ever heard of the "dress game?" I have traveled all around the world and have yet to find another family that plays this game. I always wondered where my parents got the game from. The rules were simple enough. You take an ugly dress and try to put it on the other person. Whoever was able to get the dress on the other person won the game. The loser would have to wear the dress to church that next Sunday, plain and simple.

The dress game all started because my grandmother would give my mother these ugly dresses. My mother was always big on fashion. Her closet was filled with flowing dresses with beautiful colors. My mother loved to look good. She expressed her beauty through her clothes. I'm not sure if my grandmother was trying to be funny, but she would always give my mother things she picked up while thrift shopping. But there was always one of those ugly dresses in the mix.

My grandmother would say, "Here, Cynthy, I got you a dress. How do you like it?"

It took everything in my mother not to laugh at the ridiculous designs and patterns. She always kept quiet and took the dresses. She never wanted to disrespect my grandmother. My mother always graciously accepted the dresses, no matter how hideous on or two of them were.

When my mother got home, she would laugh and complain about the clothes. Some of the dresses were too big for my mother. A few of them were draped with buttons to the floor and one of them had a huge belt on it. The dresses reminded us of clothes that somebody would give to the thrift stores knowing darn well they should have just tossed it. It would never come back in style.
My mother would look at the dresses and say, "Now, I don't know why she keeps giving me these things. I know she knows I don't wear anything like this." We all laughed with my mom and pointed at the ugly dress.

One day my grandmother gave my mom a dress that was unbearable. All of the kids were laughing at the dress and my father joined in with the jokes. The dress was so horrible and funny-looking that my house turned into a comedy club that night. My mother thought of the perfect way to get back at my father for clowning her.

While the kids were laughing, my mother inched closer to my father in the living room. She smiled innocently. All of a sudden my mother leapt on my dad and tried to put the dress over his head. They wrestled each other for control of the dress. All of the kids were cracking up laughing and pointing at the action.

"Get 'em mommy!" we yelled.

It was hysterical to see my parents battle over this dress. My mom tried to put it on my dad and my dad struggled to put it on my mom. Although my mom was so little compared to my dad, she was very strong. My mother always had that fighting spirit in her so she made it tough on him. All of the kids yelled and egged her on. We all wanted to see my mother get that dress over my daddy's head so he could wear it to church that next Sunday.

The dress game added so much fun to my house. We couldn't wait for my grandmother to give my mother a bag of clothes. No matter what it was; an ugly dress or ugly pants or even an ugly shirt, whatever it was, we knew our parents would have some fun with it. When my mother brought clothes home from my grandmother's house, we would think, "Uh oh, Mommy and Daddy 'bout to play that game."

No matter how many times they wrestled each other over those ugly dresses, no one ever won the dress game. Blame it on our big heads. As I got older, I realized that the game was never about winning or losing. It was about family time.

Turning our house into a fun factory was all that mattered to my parents. They showed us that you could have fun with your family no matter what was going on in the real world. Those wonderful days together made our family tighter. We still have fun days like that today.

There are families out there that constantly fight and have a lot of hate for each other. I cringe when I hear stories about families that shoot, stab, and even kill each other. That is not our family. We are not the type of family that gets together just for holidays and funerals. We truly enjoy being around each other. We make it a point to celebrate in fellowship. Even though we are grown-ups, every Monday is "Family Day." We try our best to never miss it. The legacy my parents received from their parents will surely be passed on to their grandchildren.

What's the point of being the Loving Family if we can't even show love to our own blood?

*

Chapter Three

"*Did you know that little black boys come from the country of Nigger (Niger) and little black girls come from the country of Niggeria (Nigeria)?*"

The misguided insult shook my young heart. I was barely seven years old but I was wise enough to know that trouble was brewing. As my younger brother, Tim, and I took the slow stroll from the bus stop to my house, we were flanked by five young white boys. Being teased by the neighborhood kids in Medford, Long Island, was nothing new for my brother and me. We didn't have many friends in the neighborhood and being mocked for the color of our skin seemed to be a weekly occurrence. I always enjoyed school but I didn't like most of the people there. Tim and I heard every insult in the book. The kids would call us anything for a laugh. Some of the students at my school even nicknamed me "chocolate milk."

I hated being teased but I was too young and afraid to put a stop to the insults. Tim and I went to the same school, Barton Elementary School. My brother found himself in the same situation. The kids in the neighborhood constantly teased him for being black. My brother was also afraid and rarely responded when the white kids in the neighborhood tried to bully him. Tim and I never ran from the mean kids in our neighborhood. We walked slowly and prayed that the kids would just leave us alone. One day the kids went too far.

"All black girls come from Niggeria," one of the boys said.

To add insult to injury, another boy repeated the tasteless slur, laughed, and then pointed at me. My brother recognized that I was scared and instinctively stepped in to protect me. He turned around and stared at the larger kids.

"If you tease us again, I am going to punch you in the face," Tim warned.

One of the larger boys didn't like the threat coming from Tim. He approached my brother and tried to intimidate him. Tim never backed down.

"I dare you," the white boy yelled. "I dare you to do something, you little nigger."

My brother went into attack mode. Tim swung and punched the white kid square in the middle of his nose. The boy's face seemed to explode like a can of red paint. He stumbled backwards and grabbed his face. The blood leaked through his pale fingers. The boy was clearly embarrassed. All of his friends became angry. They hopped off their bikes and started to tussle with Tim. I couldn't believe my eyes as I watched my brother fight what seemed to be the entire neighborhood. My brother was only in the first grade and the other boys were almost twice his size. Tim was always blessed with the mighty strength from above and he held his own as the kids jumped him. Tim never ran and he eventually fought the boys off. From that day forward, Tim never had to worry about the kids in the neighborhood putting their hands on him. He gained their respect and the racist comments seemed to go silent, at least when he was around.

Our parents never scolded Tim for protecting me. In fact, my parents encouraged it. We were always taught to look out for one another and always remain a tight unit. No matter the situation and who was the blame, we were always taught to put family first and leave outsiders on the outside. Even today, my parents constantly remind us about the importance of relying on one another.

In addition to family and education, my parents have always stressed the role of church and religion in our lives. Today, my father is an Apostolic Bishop and my mother is the Lady Elect. My parents have always been involved in the church and were never shy about teaching us the word of God. Our family went to church every week. Having biblical discussions in my house was the norm. My parents' main priority was to protect their children from the dangers of this world. That included protecting our souls.

My family's first church home was Free and Independent Holiness Church in Roosevelt, Long Island. It was in that Apostolic Church that I was taught that everything is in Jesus name. We learned that the Father, the Son and the Holy Ghost are Jesus. We were taught that God is perfect. And as promised, God had to return to the earth in the flesh as Jesus Christ to die for our sins. Without that ultimate sacrifice there would be no redemption of sin.

My first true memory of church is from when I was only three years old. Guests from Queens, New York, were visiting our church. During the sermon, I was called up by one of the visitors. The man's name was Elder Lee. He asked my parents to bring me to the front of the church.

"This child is anointed," Elder Lee said. "This child has the gift of healing. She will heal many. If not by her hand, she will heal many by her voice alone."

I was too young to understand the power of Elder Lee's prophecy. Less than a year later I was leading my first song in the same church. It was an old song called "What a Difference." The older I became the more I started to understand the responsibility of growing up in a Christian family. The last thing I wanted to do was to break the rules and suffer the eternal consequences.

My early teachings gave me a very strict outlook on life. I believed that if I wore pants or if I said a curse word or if I listened to rap music or did anything that wasn't right with the church then I would burn with the devil. Forever. I was scared to die when I was a young child. I used to believe that God was mean. My sense of religion was warped when I was younger. I didn't have a relationship with God at all. I had a relationship with the church. I was programmed. Everything I did had to revolve around pleasing God and Jesus. I knew I had to love my family but I was taught to love God first. God and Jesus are the same person, so I never wanted to make Jesus mad and burn with the devil. Forever. I used to believe that I would get struck down for having sinful thoughts. I was afraid to do anything in life. I truly believed that God would judge me for my actions and I would immediately die. It was either Holiness or Hell. Either way, I knew both were forever.

Of all the denominations of the Christian religions I know, the beliefs of the Apostolic Holiness Church were the strictest. Throughout my childhood I followed the beliefs of my parents and made sure that I didn't sin and allow the devil to corrupt my soul. I refused to curse, lie, steal, disrespect my parents or even have an impure thought when I was a kid. My mother and father laid down the law in our house and it was easy for me to follow their rules. Although I was young, the threat of losing my soul was very real to me. By watching my parents I learned how to stay protected and covered in the blood of Jesus. I wanted to live a pure life and be the perfect Christian girl. No matter how hard I strived for perfection, I soon learned that growing up in the church was no guarantee that I would be shielded from the evil that would test my family's faith.

*

Cynthia Loving

Chapter Four

When you are blessed and highly favored the enemy will always find a way to attack you and the people you love. Because I grew up in a very religious household, my family has experienced our share of spiritual attacks that could have split us apart. My father would always say that the enemy begins his attacks by focusing on the men of the family. When I was younger I didn't understand my father's words, but as I got older and began to come into the knowledge of our chosen religion I noticed that his foresight was eerily truthful. As the eldest male child in our house, it seemed that my brother, Tim, caught the most hell. For the longest time I couldn't understand why my brother was constantly getting hurt.

As a child, Tim fell off of his bike nearly a dozen times and hurt himself. I have seen my brother fall into the edge of a wooden bench and knock himself unconscious in church. It seemed that a month couldn't go by without my younger brother getting hurt. As my parents tended to Tim's constant injuries, I felt myself becoming jealous of him. Blame it on our sibling rivalry. I truly believed that Tim was purposely getting hurt just to gain my parents' attention. I was too young to understand that something deeper was happening with my brother.

One night Tim woke up and began to walk around the house. It was very late and my brother seemed to be sleepwalking. Tim stumbled around our home for a few minutes and then walked back into his bedroom. My mother heard a strange noise come from his room. It sounded like Tim was struggling and trying to scream for help. My mother rushed into his room and found Tim on the floor next to his bed. She was unsure how he had gotten there. He was struggling to breathe and my mother noticed that he was swallowing his tongue. My mother quickly rushed to his aid and saved his life. My mother prevented a horrific tragedy. No one could explain what exactly happened to my brother during that late evening. My father said it could have been something spiritual. He believed that the enemy was attacking my brother Tim again. Throughout his childhood and into his teen years, Tim had to deal with a lot of near-death experiences. I always felt that something was constantly trying to kill Tim. If the enemy's plan was to attack the strength first, Tim was the perfect target because he was clearly the strongest one of all the kids.

My parents tried their best to prepare us for life's difficulties. They constantly preached the value of staying true and never backing down when trials and tribulations surfaced to test our faith. My parents realized that we would have it tougher than the other families because of our devotion to religion. The enemy is persistent and just a few short years later it seemed that the enemy would try to destroy our family once again. This time it would happen in our very own church.

One Saturday our family was in attendance at Free and Independent Holiness Church. A bad rainstorm was tearing through the city of Roosevelt that day. Despite the weather, our church was prepared for an exciting and uplifting sermon that evening. Our church was being visited by a number of special guest speakers. My father was just a minister in the church back then. On a normal day he would have been seated with the other senior members of the congregation. This particular day he was seated in the pew with my mom and all of his kids.

A few hours into the program, my parents sensed that something was not right about the guest speakers. Although I was young I could feel the energy in the sanctuary becoming uncomfortable. People began shouting and raising their voices. I could tell that this was not a normal church service. The guest preacher was speaking against some of the beliefs of our church. A few people, including my parents, objected to the message.

I was raised in an era when people were not afraid to object to things that were said from the pulpit. Members of the congregation would immediately voice their opposition if they felt a pastor or elder was speaking out of turn. The saints in the church would yell things like "Oh, no you don't" or "Nope, that's not true." My parents were rarely vocal but this was different. My parents stood up and spiritually challenged what was being said by one of the guest speakers. My mother stood immediately, without uttering a word, you could tell that her spiritual discernment was on overdrive. She was very aware at the fact the speaker was disrespectfully trying to take over the church.

The church seemed to get louder. Back then, when things started to spin out of control in the church or when people sensed that a demon was present, the ushers would yell to get the kids removed. People in the church felt it was better to separate the children from the congregation when a spiritual conflict was ensuing. So, as the conflict escalated, someone in the church yelled, "Get the kids out of here."

Despite the unexpected chaos that night, my parents refused to back down. The heated exchange consumed the church. My mother and father continued to challenge the guest speaker. They were eventually approached by the guest speaker's ushers. Although no actual words were exchanged between the speaker and my parents, their stance and refusal to be seated was enough to prompt the ushers to try and remove my parents from the sanctuary. Even though they were faithful dues paying members, my parents were asked to leave and were eventually removed from the church. Watching my mother and father be escorted out of the sermon was heartbreaking for me. It hurt my feelings to know that the other members of the church did not come to their aid. My parents were long time members of the Free and Independent Holiness Church but they were asked to leave as if they were trespassers.

My parents never allowed that incident to weaken their faith in the church, but that service had a powerful effect on me. I started to see the church in a different light. I didn't lose faith in God, but I couldn't help but question the members of the congregation. The people I was taught to trust and believe in had turned their backs on my mother and father. For the longest time I was afraid of one day being removed from the church just like my parents. A small seed of suspicion was planted in my young mind and it was a feeling that would be hard for me to ignore. It seemed that the enemy was working on our family again and testing our faith. Little did I know that I would face a far worse demon that would alter the course of my life.

Most people consider the church congregation as their second family. We are all taught to love and support one another in spiritual fellowship. No one expects a member of their congregation to hurt them. When I was a young girl, I was subjected to a traumatizing experience. Before I was old enough to comprehend what was happening to me, I was sexually molested by a member of our church. Everyone was familiar with this young man. He was no stranger off the street. He was accepted and respected in our congregation. This young man was trusted by my parents and even allowed to spend the night in our home. During our Sunday services, people would only see one side to this young man. I witnessed a darker side to him. He was slick as a chameleon. This young man would sneak into my room like a thief in the night and rip apart the fabric of my innocence. I was traumatized by his constant violation and left with a smothering fear that kept me silent.

The physical molestation went on for some time. If he stayed with us or if our family visited his home, this young man took advantage of me behind closed doors. I was a very young girl, but I was old enough to know that what he was doing to me was dead wrong. What I didn't know was what I could do to make it stop. I was scared as hell to tell my parents. The young man's abuse eventually spun out of control and he turned his focus to my younger sister Charese.

Words will never express my hopeless feeling knowing that my sister was also being molested by him. I even pleaded with the young man to leave my sister alone but there was nothing I could do to convince him to stop.

Thank God for Charese's courage. My sister did something that I was too ashamed to do at the time. Charese spoke up. My sister told my older cousin, Sydney, about the abuse. She told Sydney that this young man was molesting us constantly. My cousin became angry and confronted the young man the following Sunday at our church.

"If you touch one of my cousins again, I swear to God, I am going to kill you!" Sydney warned him. "Touch them again and you are going to die!"

The molestation immediately ended. Although we continued to attend church with the young man, he never violated my sister or me again. The physical abuse was finally over but the emotional scars took a long time to heal. Someone that I trusted had stolen a piece of my childhood. It was difficult for me to have faith in people again. I became a shielded and guarded little girl. I was afraid to wear skirts and show my body fearing that I would be abused again. Even as I moved into my pre-teen years, I continued to hide my body. I started dressing like a tomboy. The last thing I wanted to do was entice the enemy and go through the same traumatic ordeal of being molested and taken advantage of.

That dark period in my life stayed with me for a very long time. As an adult, the effects of being molested clouded my judgment when it came to trusting men. It kept my guard up. I didn't let people into my life easily. It also has made me a warrior when it comes to protecting my daughters. I tell my kids to be mindful of the people around them. I preach the importance of speaking up if someone tries to take advantage of them or their siblings. I never want them to go through the same pain that I experienced.

Many professionals conclude that child abuse and molestation is a cycle that affects millions of people each year. The odds are high that my abuser also was abused. In 2013, my sister Charese and I received a message from him. Our abuser told me that it was impossible for him to move on with his life because of what he had done to us. He apologized to us and said that he was sorry for the physical and emotional turmoil he put us through. Today he is a preacher. He is married and has children. There were rumors that he was molested by a member of his own family. Despite the immeasurable pain that I've suffered as a result of his actions, I have accepted his apology and have since forgiven him. I pray that the cycle of abuse that violated our family back then has been broken.

I thank God that we never became abusers. Respect for life and the innocence of childhood has always been important to us. The enemy that my father warned us about tried to use the hands of a trusted friend to destroy us, but Charese's courage and Sydney's protection proved that no enemy is strong enough to defeat a family that is bound tightly by love.

*

Cynthia Loving

Chapter Five

Growing up in a Christian household has taught me many things. I learned about the importance of love for family. I learned how to be obedient and respectful to my elders. I even learned how to be forgiving and understanding when things didn't go my way. Despite all the knowledge that was passed down to me, nothing could prepare me for being abused at such an earlier age. I didn't realize it at the time, but my silence spoke volumes. During my childhood, many awful things occurred between church-folks. Infidelity, dishonesty, drug abuse, theft, cheating, gossiping, and child abuse was prevalent. In an effort to save face, many things were swept under the rug. Most of the foolishness was going on right under everyone's noses, but the truth was forever lost because silence ruled the day.

As a young girl, just barely entering into my double-digit years, I found my own way to cope with being abused. While many young girls were experimenting with skirts, dresses and makeup I was becoming a recluse and dressing like a boy more than a young woman. As my body changed, I didn't want anyone to see my shape so I often wore my brother's or my cousin's clothes. The little innocent girl that most people knew as Lil' Cindy was slowly fading into the background. I didn't want to be hurt again. I didn't want anyone to touch Lil' Cindy so I started to add an edge to my personality. I spoke less in public and stayed by myself most times. People thought I was a shy tomboy. In reality, I was simply on guard.

Right in the middle of this identity crisis, music was becoming a big part of my life. I continued to lead songs in church and started finding my voice. When I was alone in my room I wrote songs and poetry. When I got really bored I lined up my dolls and held talent shows by myself. Sometimes my siblings joined in the fun. I enjoyed singing and performing. I knew I wanted to be a singer and a superstar and as I got older I gained more confidence in my God given talents. I was only allowed to sing gospel songs back then. I imitated The Clark Sisters and The Winans. They were my first inspiration. My parents didn't allow us to listen to Rap music. My mom and dad tried to keep us protected from all the cursing and sexual references. My parents only let us hear a few R&B songs but Rap music was not allowed in our home.

No matter how hard my parents tried to protect us, there was no way they could keep us away from the exploding Rap Music phenomenon known as Hip-Hop. It was everywhere. The late 80s and early 90s was the golden era of rap music. It seemed as if everyone was listening to it. From the first time I heard the rough, ghetto sound, I loved it. I was seductively drawn to the rebellious nature of the music. I couldn't believe the rappers were brave enough to talk about things that I was too afraid to even think about. Big Daddy Kane, Salt-N-Pepa, and MC Lyte were some of my favorites. I listened to the music when I was in school or at a friend's house. I couldn't get enough of the raw sound. Hip-Hop went against everything I learned in the church. The rappers were so defiant! They seemed to question authority with every verse. The more rebellious the rapper and the music, the more I loved it.

My older cousin, Sydney, was also a huge fan of Hip-Hop music and the culture. My parents would allow us to listen to a few Hip-Hop records when he would visit us. My mom and dad trusted Sydney. They knew he would make sure that we didn't listen to anything that was out of control. My cousin introduced me to a lot of underground rap music that I didn't hear on the radio back then. We heard a lot of rappers from New York and the culture started to consume me. I admired the way they dressed and the jewelry they wore. I started to emulate the rappers that I read about in the magazines and heard on the radio.

As I got older I picked up on the exploding Hip-Hop fashion as well. I wore leather kufi-hats and baggy clothes like the rappers. When we visited our family in Roosevelt, Long Island, I wore my cousin's graffiti jacket and big sweaters. I wore fake gold teeth made out of Rolo candy paper. I even asked my god-sister to dye my hair with orange Kool-Aid, so I could look like the rappers. I would do anything to be connected to the culture. When a new magazine was released I would sneak into the store and flip through the pages. I was never allowed to bring the magazines home but that didn't stop me from sneaking a peek whenever possible. Sometimes I even found myself writing letters to the artists' fan clubs.

They were so cool. I wanted to learn everything about them. I wanted them to be my friend.

    Hip-Hop music had a profound effect on me when I was a young girl. As I explored deeper into the culture, I wanted to learn more. I respected my parents' wishes and never listened to the music in the house. I waited until I got to school or stayed at a friend's house to get my Hip-Hop fix. I knew I was being defiant at the time but I would never do anything to disrespect my parents or their house rules. Hip-Hop gave me a much different outlook on life than what I was used to. The confidence and swagger of the artists impressed me. I wanted to be confident and brave like them. Hip-Hop helped me suppress the fear I was experiencing as a result of the abuse I had suffered. In the beginning, I just buried my body behind the big clothes. After a while, I hid Lil' Cindy behind the Hip-Hop culture and started to create a new identity.

*

Chapter Six

By the time I was twelve years old I noticed things in my family beginning to change. My father joined the military and my parents decided to leave New York. We were far from becoming a dysfunctional family but not having my father around had a visible effect on us. When we lived on Long Island it seemed that we were protected and safe. Most of our family lived within a few miles and we always felt covered. From the moment we moved to Texas, it felt like we had slipped into the Twilight Zone. When my father left for Korea we moved from Fort Hood, Texas, to Atlanta, Georgia. For the first time in my life I was living in a place outside of New York. I was also living without my father.

While my dad was overseas and making a living to feed his family, my mother seemed to work around the clock and did everything she could to keep our family tight. She continued her career as a school teacher while my father was starting a new one in the military. My dad was gone for months at a time but it felt like years to us. He called home whenever he could and my mother exchanged long letters with him. My dad even surprised us by coming home a few times a year. We always were excited to see him and hated when he had to leave again.

Our family was different when my dad was not around. The consistency that comes with having two parents in our family unit was gone. Despite the enormous challenges she faced, my mother managed to keep our house in order with four children. No matter how tough things were, my mother didn't play when it came to raising her family. There were plenty of things my mother didn't tolerate and one of them was a dirty home. While most kids spent their Saturdays watching cartoons and eating cereal, my mother made it mandatory for all of her children to do "major cleanup" around the house. She never got much of a fight out of us because her word was the law.

Although we had a lot of fun when we were younger, we were rarely allowed to do much outside of the house. My mother wanted us to go to school, maintain excellent grades and follow the rules of the Bible. She didn't allow us to spend the night out and no one was allowed to stay with us unless my mother knew their family. My mother wasn't a tyrant with her rules but she was far from a pushover. She needed to be strict to keep us protected. She didn't want anyone to know that my father wasn't around. Her main priority has always been family. She worked hard to keep us sheltered and protected. As my father was transferred to different locations across the world we found ourselves moving from city to city back here in the States. We eventually moved to Fort Bragg in North Carolina.

Without the strong male presence in the house, my siblings and I began to act out. We never did anything to disrespect my mother but we started to test the limits. As I grew older, and bolder, I began to buck up against the house rules more and more. One day I would defy my mother and she would make me pay the consequences.

I was attending E.E. Smith High School in Fayetteville, North Carolina, at the time. I knew a lot of kids from my school and I had a number of friends. There were a few male friends in my circle but I was not allowed to have a boyfriend. My mother always reminded me that sex was for married people. She even warned me not to kiss any boys fearing that I would entice them to expect more from me. My mother was very serious about her rules. She always told me that she possessed a good intuition and she knew what was best for me. Most times, I would take her advice without question, but, when I felt my mother was just being mean, I disobeyed and ignored her rules.

During my first year of high school, I was friends with a boy named David. My mother had met David on a number of occasions. She did not like him at all. David was a bad boy. That's what I liked about him. He didn't attend E.E. Smith High and he was older than me. One day, my mother sat me down to have a discussion about my new friend.

"I don't want you talking to him. He is bad news," my mother said referring to David. "Every time he comes around it just seems like nothing good is going to come from that situation."

I got frustrated with my mother. I felt like she didn't want me to be happy. I didn't heed her warning and I continued to talk to my new friend.

One day, David called my school and pretended to be my father. He called looking for me and said that he was Sergeant Loving. For security reasons the school contacted my mother and told her that someone called the school pretending to be my father.

    I didn't have a clue about what David had done. My friend waited until I got home after school and he stopped by to see me. We were laughing and joking on the porch when my mother got home from work. As she walked to the front door I knew something was wrong. The cold look on her face made me nervous. I immediately thought back to when she told me not to talk to David again. I wanted to explain to her that my friend was really a good guy. His grandmother was in church and my mother just needed to get to know him better. By the look on her face I could tell that my mother had no intentions of allowing me to see him again.

    "Come in the house for a second," my mother calmly said and walked inside.

    "Okay," I replied.

    I sensed that my mother was upset. I left David on the front porch and headed inside the house. I didn't know what to expect but I started preparing myself to defend my actions. I walked inside my bedroom and my mother was waiting for me.

    "Yeah, what's up?" I nervously asked.

    "I thought I told you not to have that boy at my house?" my mother asked. "I told you he's bad news."

    "What are you talking about?" I immediately snapped. "I didn't even do nothing."

    Getting smart with my mother was the last mistake I made that day. She quickly lost all of her patience with me and lashed out. I'm not sure if it was a right hook, a left hook, an uppercut or a drop kick that almost knocked me unconscious. Before I could run out of the room, my mother grabbed a hold of me and started beating my ass. I couldn't believe it.

"Oh, my God!" I yelled. "Let me go."

My dad was home that day and witnessed everything that happened. I remember screaming for him to get my mother off of me. He shook his head at me.

"That is between y'all," my dad said. "I'm not getting involved."

My mother continued to pounce on me while all of my siblings watched.

"Oh, my God, mommy is beatin' up Cindy!" one of them yelled.

I tried to pull away from my mother but she was too strong. She was clearly upset that I tried to buck up against her and she wanted to make sure that I learned my lesson. I grew up in a time when parents were not afraid to knock their kids out. The threat of protective services never fazed them. My mother would always say that if protective services came to our house then they would get their butts beat too.

With every punch from my mother I learned that she didn't play when it came to her rules. Before she could hit me again I finally broke away from her and ran out of the bedroom. My mother's anger had scared me beyond belief. I had never seen her so upset with me and I was ready to get the hell out of Dodge. I bolted through the house and ran outside.

"You better leave!" I yelled at David. "My mom is crazy!"

David didn't ask any questions. He recognized that I was in trouble for having him around and he decided to leave. I guess he didn't want to feel the wrath of my mother. When David left from my house that day, it was the last time

I ever saw him.

It turned out that my mother's intuition about David was correct. Later that school year, David found himself in some trouble. He was shot multiple times during an altercation. I heard that he died as a result. I couldn't believe my ears when I received the news. Ironically, my mother's strict rules had saved me from a world of trouble and, possibly, saved my life.

No matter how much I tried to rebel against my mother's rules I respected the fact that she was always looking out for me. The book of Exodus reminds us to honor our mother and father so that our days may be long. It's true that my parents would get on my nerves when I was a teen but I would never disrespect them fearing that God would cut me short.

As I got older my mother continued to protect me with her rules. When I wanted to go to a party I asked for her permission. Sometimes she would tell me that she didn't have a good feeling about an event and she would forbid me from attending. Although I was upset it seemed that her intuition was always correct. The next day I would find out that someone got shot or stabbed at the party and I would feel grateful that I wasn't there.

I respect and rely on my mother's intuition to this day. I learned some valuable lessons from her strict rules. I can't thank my mother enough for being hard on me even when I didn't understand why. Her tough ways eventually rubbed off on me. I often relied on my mother's hard lessons to handle my business and navigate through my everyday life. I have never seen my mother back down from a fight or a challenge. My mother is a sweet person but she also has a quick switch that makes her turn into a super thug from the Andrew Jackson Projects in the South Bronx if the situation calls for it. She never accepted excuses from her children and failure was never an option. I'm not sure if I would be the person I am today without my mother's spiritual guidance and heavy hand that kept me on the straight and narrow.

Cynthia Loving

Chapter Seven

I knew at an early age that I was going to be an entertainer. Leading songs in church and using my voice to praise God gave me a sense of spirituality and reverence. My family moved around a lot when we left New York, but no matter which city we called our home my mother kept us in the church. Gospel music gave me a great foundation to develop my voice and to find my style.

Despite going to church every week I was still carrying on my love affair with Hip-Hop. I wasn't allowed to listen to the songs in the house but I did whatever I needed to do to keep up with the new music and fashion. As I got older, I started to listen to more hardcore Hip-Hop. While the veteran rappers of the late 80s were making songs about self-destruction and fighting the power, the early 90s were giving birth to a new breed of MC. The new rappers were making songs about street life and violence. The gritty new sound grabbed me. The vivid storytelling and graphic nature of the music was captivating. It was nothing like I had ever experienced. In 1992, I heard about a rapper who would change everything for me. From the first time I saw him on television, I knew that I wanted to grow up and be exactly like this thugged-out rapper.

    Tupac Shakur exploded onto the rap scene in the early 1990s. His authentic appeal and powerful vocals were a strong combination that a lot of rappers couldn't duplicate. I was hooked from the moment I heard "Brenda's Got a Baby" and "Keep Your Head Up." Tupac wasn't afraid to touch on the harsh topics of life in the ghetto. He had a rough style but he was also real. When I watched Tupac play his infamous character "Bishop" in the movie "Juice," it was over for me. I wanted to be exactly like Tupac. I made up my mind that I was going to add the rap element to my style. I looked up to a lot of rappers when I was a teenager but none of them had a more profound effect on me than Tupac Shakur.

    I started writing more rhymes in my spare time. I didn't have a lot of instrumentals back then, so I wrote my raps when there was a break in the songs. I let people hear my lyrics and freestyled verses for them. There were other rappers in my school. Sometimes we had one-on-one competitions. I battled dudes in the lunchroom or after classes. I crushed them. I got better and better at rapping and I started to feel like I was a part of the culture. As my skills improved, I jumped at any opportunity to show off my talent. One day while I was attending E.E. Smith High School, my friends, Bardell Berry, Kevin Scott, and I decided to participate in an upcoming talent show. I felt excited about the chance to showcase our rapping skills. We decided to perform the song "Where I'm From" by Digable Planets. For the next few weeks, I woke up earlier than usual so that we could rehearse before school started. Bardell, Kevin, and I worked hard until we got the verses and dance routines down to perfection. Our performance was going to be amazing.

A few days before the talent show, our makeshift rap group was hit with some bad news. Kevin had gotten himself into trouble. He was suspended from school. I was devastated when I found out that Kevin couldn't participate in the show. It would be impossible for Bardell and me to do the song without our third member. We considered adding another person to replace Kevin, but no one could duplicate the chemistry we had created. I couldn't believe that all of our hard work and dedication was about to be washed away. As fate would have it, the school had a change of heart. We were contemplating canceling our performance when we received word that Kevin would be allowed to perform in the talent show. It was exciting. We performed at the talent show. All of the kids in the crowd loved it. We added an insane dance routine to our act and were rewarded with a thunderous round of applause. The feeling was indescribable.

My normal routine for a talent show would have been a gospel song, but after the amazing response I received from rapping on stage I knew I had to keep the Hip-Hop element in my act. My style was lyrical and creative. People were immediately drawn to my New York style and they loved to hear me rap. Ironically, it would be my love for the Hip-Hop culture that would help me land my very first singing gig with a well-known gospel artist.

Despite the love I was getting at school for my Hip-Hop performance, I was still concealing that side of me from my family. Hip-Hop went against most things I learned in the church and I didn't want my parents to discover that I was involved in the culture. If my dad found out that I was rapping he would immediately have conducted a prayer circle around me to convince me to stop. By my junior in high school, my love for Hip-Hop was too deep to hide. I started rapping and singing openly and people started to know me for my versatility. I was finally coming out of my shell.

Later that year, I received the news that my uncle, John P. Kee, was looking for background singers for his upcoming tour. John P. Kee was already a huge star in the gospel music world. His hit records were heavily played on radio stations nationwide. His tour would be a great opportunity for me if I was selected. I would finally get a taste of the entertainment business and see what it was like to perform on the road. Although we were family, my uncle made me audition for the position. I didn't mind at all because I was excited to show him what I could do. I decided not to sing for the audition. Instead, I freestyled a verse and did a dance move for them. I remembered watching a rap group called "Kid N' Play". They would jump over their legs in their music videos. I did the same dance move in my audition. Everyone in the room went crazy. My uncle was very impressed with me and gave me the job.

My father was very supportive of my decision to sing background for my uncle. My dad would make the three hour drive to Charlotte and take me to rehearsal at least twice per week. Even when our rehearsals would run late into the night my father would stay with me to make sure I got back to Fayetteville for school the next day. I could never thank my dad enough for making those sacrifices for me. Singing with my uncle paved the way for countless opportunities in the music industry. Performing on the road was a wonderful experience. I was young, vibrant, making money, and doing something that I loved.

After getting my first taste of the industry and performing on tour, it was time for me to think long and hard about becoming an artist. I had started out by watching hundreds of music videos and emulating other rappers and singers. Now, I needed to create a sound and a look that people would never forget. My good friend, Renee LaGoff, and I always discussed how to create that signature look. Renee was also a background singer for my uncle. She introduced me to a lot of people in the industry. One day while we were on break, Renee asked me about my career. She wanted to know my plans for introducing myself as an artist.

"When you make it big you will need to have a name that people can chant," Renee said. "Just in case the crowd wants you to come back out for an encore, your name has to be something that people can remember and easily scream. Do you want them to yell out Cindy Loving?"

Until that day, I had never settled on a serious artist name. When I was younger, I went by "Little Cindy" and "Young Wisdom" in school. While I was on tour with John P. Kee people would call me "Monie" because I reminded them of Monie Love. I didn't have a problem with people calling me "Monie" because she was a huge inspiration to me as I developed my rapping style. I wasn't going to use "Monie" so I needed to come up with an original stage name.

Renee recognized that my style was more on the Hip-Hop side. She said that I reminded her of a Mary J. Blige type of singer with a Hip-Hop vibe to me. She said my name needed to be cool but edgy. I was a huge fan of Lil' Kim at the time and a light bulb went off in my head. I loved the fact that

Lil' Kim was short like me and her sound was raw.

"What about Lil' Mo or something like that?" I asked.

"That's hot!" Renee quickly responded.

"What? Lil' Mo? You like that?" I asked.

"Yes. Lil' Mo! That's hot," Renee smiled. "It's a perfect name to blend the Hip-Hop and R&B together."

My friend's reaction was all that I needed. I had officially found my stage name. *Lil' Mo* was derived from a perfect blend of two artists that I absolutely adored and respected. I wanted the creative vibe of Monie Love and the raw sound of Lil' Kim to be evident in my songs. That innocent conversation changed the course of my life. Everything felt right about my decision. I couldn't wait to make it back to Fayetteville.

When I arrived in North Carolina, my first stop was the tattoo parlor. There were plenty of tattoo spots in the Fort Bragg area. Normally, the artist would have rejected my request for an appointment. I was under the age of eighteen but I was driving at the time. I told the artist that I left my identification home and they agreed to do my first tattoo. After signing the waivers and paying the fifty dollars, I sat down in the chair and made it official. My first tattoo was only a few inches wide but it would have a momentous effect on my life. As I looked down at the finished ink on my arm, I knew that things would never be the same. The name "Lil Mo" was now etched deep into my skin but the person seemed to be lying dormant within me my entire life. It was now time to introduce the world to *Lil' Mo*.

*

PART II
Meet the Girl Next Door

Chapter Eight

"*...It's better to marry than to burn.*"

That profound scripture stuck with me since I was old enough to understand its meaning. Before I graduated from high school, the temptation of sex was the furthest thing from my mind. I had a laser focus on my schoolwork and was ready to graduate early. I also was doing hair at the time and making decent money for my age. While I kept my head buried in my books and focused on my GPA, a lot of girls in my school were experimenting with sex. Rumors and gossip spread throughout the building but I was naïve to the subject. When I heard the stories about how someone was "sleeping with" another person, I thought they were referring to sleeping in the same bed. I had no clue that people were talking about sex.

Growing up in the *Loving* household had a profound effect on the way I viewed relationships, sex and marriage. My mother was completely committed to my father. My parents were never separated and never divorced. I never knew my mother to be with another man and that was my plan as well. I believed that my first boyfriend would be my first love, my only love. I believed that I would marry him and give him everything. Before I entered high school, I made two promises to myself: I wouldn't use profanity before graduation and I wouldn't have sex. I remained engrossed in my studies and steered clear of letting boys dictate my world. Although I dressed like a tomboy in high school, a few boys found me attractive and tried to talk to me. Despite their attempts to get close to me, I refused to let my guard down. Like any typical teenage girl, I had a number of friends at school but I never allowed anything to escalate beyond a friendship.

    My life started to change drastically during my final year of high school. At sixteen, I was one of the youngest seniors in my high school. My grades were outstanding and I was excelling in all subjects. My focus and determination was paying off. With my senior year coming to an end, the last thing on my mind was becoming somebody's girlfriend. That would all change when one of my friends introduced me to a boy from New York. He was a rugged young man who wore gold teeth, now referred to as "grills." A typical New Yorker, he always kept a tight, low haircut. His stocky build was all muscle like a running back. He dressed like a rapper and his demeanor was painted with a Hip-Hop flavor. I was instantly drawn to him. His name was "Brooklyn."

    It didn't take long for Brooklyn and me to become a couple. We grew very close, very quickly. Before long, I started to believe that I was going to spend the rest of my life with him. We both were young but it felt like we had known each other for years. Brooklyn was a typical bad boy. I liked that about him. He was known as a troublemaker at his school and had been kicked out repeatedly for fighting. I was blown away by his brashness.

I was young and impressionable and Brooklyn seemed to appease my appetite for boys that reminded me of Tupac Shakur. Our relationship started as an innocent fling. Although Brooklyn was from New York, he lived near Fayetteville with his family and we saw each other often. Our relationship started building and my affection for him grew stronger every day. As I learned more about Brooklyn and his issues, I felt compelled to care for him and stay by his side. When he needed something I tried my best to accommodate him. Brooklyn was my first real boyfriend and I was willing to do anything and everything to make it work.

After dating for a few months, our conversations started shifting to the subject of sex. Brooklyn knew I was still a virgin but I was adamant about not having sex before I graduated high school. Trying to wait until marriage seemed so impossible. That didn't stop Brooklyn from constantly giving me advice about sex. I remember Brooklyn warning me that my first time would hurt worse if I waited too long to lose my virginity. He also told me that if I had sex at an early age that it would make it easier for my body to be prepared to have a child. I had no clue whether or not Brooklyn was lying to me. I tried to learn as much as I could about sex but I knew there was nothing like experiencing it for myself. Some of my older friends were having sex and I knew some of my god-sisters were doing it. I started to feel like I was missing out. The more I heard about sex and the more Brooklyn and I discussed the topic, the more curious I became.

My family never discussed the birds and the bees in detail in my house. My mother and father always warned me about the Bible's stance on fornication. They wanted me to save myself for marriage. My parents knew that a lot of young girls were having sex but they never sat me down and told me what to expect when I finally decided to lose my virginity. While my parents were relatively quiet about the topic, my boyfriend never hesitated to tell me everything he knew. Brooklyn schooled me all the time and let me pick his brain about sex. I trusted him and believed everything he told me. No matter how ridiculous his advice sounded, my young mind soaked it up.

One day while we were having a discussion, Brooklyn said to me, "You know if you have sex with me, your titties and your butt will get big."

Instead of questioning Brooklyn, I listened to him and tried my best to learn as much as I could. It didn't take long for me to realize that Brooklyn had an ulterior motive with all of his sex talk. No matter how many discussions we had, I would never succumb to Brooklyn's temptation and go against my promise. He was my boyfriend and I wanted to give him everything. I was ready to share my love with him but I wanted to make sure the time was right.

A few months later, I graduated high school with honors. I had accomplished all of my goals and I was ready to start the next chapter in my life. Brooklyn and I had grown very close during my senior year. Our relationship felt natural. I trusted him with everything, including my heart. Brooklyn was my first love. My feelings for him were undeniable. I was growing more curious about sex with each passing day. I refused to be the only person who was clueless about the experience. Brooklyn had gained my love and later that summer I decided that he would be the first and only man to have my body. I had finally made up my mind. I was ready to lose my virginity. I would let Brooklyn take the only stroll through my enchanted garden.

Leading up to the big day, Brooklyn seemed to say all of the right things. He was very nice and considerate and tried to accommodate me every step of the way. He suggested that we meet at his cousin's house so that we could be alone. I agreed. I felt nervous about my decision but I trusted that Brooklyn would make my first experience a memorable one. He gave me the directions to his cousin's house and I drove right over. There was no turning back now. I was finally going to have my own story to tell.

When I arrived to his cousin's house I felt nervous. Brooklyn was alone and he invited me inside. He offered me something to drink and tried to make me comfortable. He didn't want me to feel rushed, but I could tell he was anxious. He walked me to the bedroom and we talked for a few minutes. The talking turned into kissing and before I knew it Brooklyn and I were messing around. I tried to get lost in the moment but I was still nervous.

I love you," Brooklyn whispered to me. "I'm so glad that you are my girlfriend."

Brooklyn's words made me smile. I believed him and started to feel more comfortable. By professing his love to me, Brooklyn made me trust him even more. I knew that I was about to give him something that I could never take back. His soft words erased all of my doubt and I knew then that I was making the right decision.

"Do you have any protection?" I asked.

"Oh, yea, I do," Brooklyn quickly responded. "But you probably won't need it because it's your first time.

Protection is only for people that don't want to get pregnant. You don't have to worry about that because you never had sex before."

"Oh, okay," I said.

Because I was so young and inexperienced, I didn't think to question his response. Brooklyn never got a condom and we decided to have unprotected sex. He laid me down on my back and undressed me. He told me to open my legs and keep still as he started to penetrate my very soul.

When I was a young girl, I dreamed that my first time would be something out of a fairy tale. I imagined that I would be in a plush bedroom with white linen sheets and gorgeous pillows. I dreamed that there would be sexy R&B music playing in the bedroom. Maybe even a song by Luther Vandross. I imagined that I would walk into a palace-type room and my man would be eagerly awaiting me. He would grab me gently and twirl me around while my clothes graciously fell to the floor. He would kiss all over my body and make me feel like I was the only woman on earth. I dreamed that my first time would be full of love and passion. I imagined it would be like one of those movies on the Playboy or Cinemax channels. I just knew that my first love would make me moan with desire. I would be with him until the end of time.

My first time was nothing like the fairy tales I had imagined. I couldn't believe how much pain I was in as Brooklyn struggled to enter me. It felt nothing like I anticipated. It didn't feel affectionate or soft like the moment when Brooklyn said he loved me. I thought my first experience was going to send chills up my spine but there were no chills. There was only pain. It felt like the excruciating feeling was never going to end.

"Wait. We have to stop," I moaned.

"I'm halfway there now," Brooklyn responded.

Halfway? I thought to myself. He continued to push himself inside and I held on for dear life. Brooklyn tried to coach me through the experience but I couldn't ignore the pain.

"I forgot to tell you," Brooklyn said. "Because this is your first time, you are probably going to bleed."

"Bleed? What do you mean?" I gasped. "Oh, my God! If I bleed my mother is going to find out what I did."

"Don't worry about it. I'm in now," Brooklyn said.

I couldn't believe how things were unfolding. All I could do was try my best to enjoy myself. I tried to act like I was in love and this was the best day of my life but the pain and the awkwardness was unbearable. It felt like we were at it for an eternity as I lay there. Brooklyn finally finished and rolled off of me. My body felt numb as the room fell silent. I didn't know what to say. I thought about the painful experience of losing my virginity. A rush of emotion came over me and I started to feel guilty and ashamed.

"I really don't feel comfortable right now," I whispered to Brooklyn.

He turned over and looked at me. I expected my boyfriend to comfort me and tell me that he loved me again.

"Well, you don't have to worry about me asking for that again," Brooklyn blurted.

"Huh?" I shockingly responded. "What does that mean?"

"You don't have to worry about me asking for that again," Brooklyn repeated.

"You don't even know what the hell you are doing. You are bleeding all over the place. This is my cousin's house. We have to clean this shit up."

Brooklyn's unexpected mood swing shocked me. I was hurt and confused. Brooklyn got up and started cleaning up the bedroom. I tried to regain my composure and helped him pull the sheets off the bed. We had undoubtedly made a mess and it was enough to make me question my decision. It was hard for me to believe that this experience was what all the girls were raving about. I cringed at the thought of what I had to look forward to. The guilt and the shame inside of me began to build. I had lost my virginity to Brooklyn and now he was the man I was going to be with. I knew that I went against my religious beliefs by allowing this to happen but I believed that my sins would go into remission if we eventually became a married couple.

Brooklyn began to act differently after we had sex. We were still a couple but I could tell that something inside of him had changed. Brooklyn knew that he was my first love and that no one would ever have my body besides him. I started to feel like he owned me. Despite all of his talk about not asking me for sex again, Brooklyn called me just a few days later and asked if I was ready to go at it again. I never denied him because he was my boyfriend. I thought I was obligated to do whatever I had to do to make him happy.

Later that summer, Brooklyn moved back to New York City. We barely stayed in contact. I eventually moved to New York to live with my Aunt Barbie. Despite living just a train ride away, Brooklyn and I hardly saw each other. He never made his way to my side of town to visit. I always travelled to him but he refused to head out to Queens to meet me. I didn't understand why he never made an effort to see me. I was his girlfriend. I do know that the beef between boroughs was still alive, but I felt this could have been my Romeo & Juliet love story moment. Come to me by any means necessary. Show your love. Prove to me this is why I gave you my cherry. There are no do-overs once it's popped. I had a gut feeling of what was to come. I didn't want to accept it, but there was no getting around it.

Brooklyn and I drifted apart. I was so disappointed with myself. For the longest time I resented my decision to lose my virginity that summer. I hated the fact that I didn't wait. Now that I was single and alone I had to deal with the reality of making a terrible mistake. I went against my better judgment and I asked God for forgiveness. I never spoke to my parents about my situation. I didn't want my mother and father to be ashamed of me. My guilt slowly grew into a heavy burden and I fell into a slight depression. I felt like a walking disgrace. I was paranoid whenever I found myself around people. I thought everyone knew that I was no longer a virgin. When I saw people talking and joking, I just knew that they were talking about me. The heavy stain of being deflowered stuck with me for a long time. I didn't want to have sex with anyone else and I had no clue how to shake the guilt. I felt lost, devastated. I needed to move on.

Later that year, my outlook on the future started to change. I continued to pursue my music career and I kept my eye on hair school. My relationship with Brooklyn had been dead for some time, but I had started to regain my confidence. I was still skeptical about meeting new people but I knew that I had to find a way to not become a recluse.

A few weeks later I found myself on a video set for the

rap group Gang Starr. I was with my good friend, "G," who was the stepbrother of the group's DJ. He played a major role in hooking me up with my first gig on the Jazzmatazz Tour. I was still leery about being around people but I felt comfortable knowing that he was there. I met a great guy from Long Island named DJ Dummy. It was cool to learn that we had ties in Nassau County. We immediately hit it off. We shared some of the same experiences and we were both familiar with each other's churches. We hung out on the set the entire day.

Later that evening, I noticed a young man looking my way while DJ Dummy and I were talking. I wasn't in the mood to holler at anyone so I became nervous. The young man continued to look my way and walked over to me. As he got closer his face started to look familiar.

"Excuse me," the young man said. "Are you Cindy Loving?"

My jaw immediately dropped the minute I heard his voice. I smiled. I couldn't believe my eyes. I hadn't seen him since we attended Deer Park Elementary School together but I instantly recognized the young man. His name was Vee.

"Oh, my God. It's a small world. What are you doing here?" I asked.

"My man's baby-mother takes pictures of the video sets," Vee said. "We are a rap group and we're trying to get a cameo in the video."

"Oh, okay," I said with a smile.

Vee and I talked for the rest of the evening. Having Vee close to me on the video set immediately made me feel safe. Vee helped to take my mind off the personal battle I was having with my guilt. Even though we spent a brief time on the set together, I was grateful for his presence. We exchanged numbers that night and eventually started a cool friendship. I felt like myself again when I was with Vee. I felt emotionally free. Vee had an uncanny knack for making me forget about the issues I had with Brooklyn and all the heavy baggage I was bringing from that failed relationship. As Vee and I spent more time together, the heavy burden I was carrying began to lift. Vee never hesitated to pick me up in his own car and take me out. He made me feel loved.

That summer would be the last time Brooklyn and I would see each other. We lost contact for many years after our breakup. I remained close with a few of his relatives but we never laid eyes on each other again. The relationship we had taught me a lot of valuable lessons that have remained with me. I learned that life happens and sometimes things will not go as smooth as we plan them. I thank God that I didn't succumb to the burden of guilt that I placed on myself at such an early age. Before losing my virginity to Brooklyn, I had planned for him to be my only lover, but us being together forever was never in Brooklyn's plans.

Life has a funny way of humbling us all when we least expect it. A few years ago I received an inbox message from Brooklyn. He reached out to me on Facebook. I was surprised to hear from him. Brooklyn told me that he was happy for my success. He said he was proud to see that I was doing well and that he was following my career. Brooklyn went on to tell me that he changed his life around. He said he was working and getting his life back in order. He apologized for the drama he took me through during that summer after I graduated high school. He said that he was young and that he was going through a lot of personal issues. His regret seemed heartfelt. I responded that I accepted his apology.

About a year later Brooklyn reached out to me again through Facebook. When I saw his name in my inbox I tried to imagine why he was reaching out again. I was expecting another apology or even an attempt to reconcile. When I read his message I was at a total loss for words.

"Hey, I'm sorry to bother you. I hope this email finds you well," Brooklyn said. "I know you used to always say that I was going to need you before you was going to need me. Well, the time has come in my life when I do need you. Do you have like $3,000 I can borrow? And, if I can, I will tell you where you can send it. If you don't reply to this message then I can take a hint. Either way, be blessed."

I read the message a few times to make sure I was reading it correctly. I never responded to the email. Since the day I met him, Brooklyn has always felt the need to teach me and school me about life. I learned many lessons from Brooklyn, good ones and bad ones. I can take away a jewel to better my life even from his final message to me. I'm grateful for the relationship I had with him. Going through the good times and the bad times has taught me a lot. To overcome physical, mental and emotional pain is a triumph. I will always show genuine love and for that I am and will continue to *be blessed.*

*

Chapter Nine

"*You're pregnant!*"

The words hit me harder than a sledge hammer. Being pregnant was the last thing I expected to hear when I visited the local hospital in Fayetteville, North Carolina. For the past few weeks I hadn't been feeling well. The constant vomiting left me thinking I was suffering from a stomach virus. After a few days of putting it off, I pulled myself together and headed to the hospital to see what was going on. After a brief examination that included a pregnancy test, I was hit with the bombshell. My sister was sitting next to me and immediately started laughing at the shocking news. My reaction totally was the opposite. I burst into tears. The news felt surreal to me. I was still in my teens and a million years away from being ready for a child. I was not financially stable nor was I emotionally ready to handle the pressure of starting my own family. The first thing that flashed in my mind was how disappointed my parents were going to be when they heard the news.

When I was a young girl I imagined this moment would be different. The last thing I wanted to be was somebody's baby-mother. I was still dating my boyfriend Vee but our relationship was not as strong as it once was. I was living in Queens, New York, at the time with my Aunt Barbie. My boyfriend Vee had been having a tough time in New York so he decided to move to Atlanta. We saw each other when we could, but I knew our relationship was fading. Getting the news that I was pregnant put a new twist on our relationship. My mother and father didn't know a lot about Vee and hadn't seen him since we were schoolmates back at Deer Park Elementary School. How would I find the courage to tell them that I was knocked up? The last thing I wanted to do was to shame the *Loving* name by having their first grandchild out of wedlock.

When I got back to my parents' house I went straight to my room and closed the door. I didn't want them to see me at all so I tried to hide. I was only visiting my parents in North Carolina for a few more days. Soon I would be heading back to New York but I knew eventually I would have to tell them the results of my test.

Little did I know that while I lay crying in my room, Charese was breaking the news to my parents. They immediately wanted to talk to me so I swallowed my fear and told them everything that was going on. I was shocked by their reaction. My father tried his best to stay positive and my mother immediately became supportive of me and my situation. They didn't yell at me nor did they try to make me feel bad. I could tell that they were disappointed that I was now facing a major change in my life, but despite the shocking news, they reassured me that they would be there for me. My mother suggested that I tell my aunt so she wouldn't be blindsided when I returned to New York. I took my mother's advice and called my Aunt Barbie.

"Heeyyyyyy!" My aunt answered the phone with her usual vibrant voice. "When are you coming back to New York?"

"Well, I'll be coming back soon." I responded in a soft voice again searching for the courage to break the news. "But I just wanted to let you know that I'm pregnant."

"Oh wow," Aunt Barbie responded, "Oh, my God, have you told your mother yet? I just don't want her to think that I let you come up here and run buck wild."

"Yes, I told my mom," I said. "My mother told me to call you to tell you the news. I will probably have to move in with my boyfriend if need be."

"Oh, no. You don't have to do that," my aunt reassured me, "Whatever we have to do. You can always stay here."

I was surprised at how supportive my family was. I knew my family was hurt and somewhat upset by my decisions but everyone seemed to put their personal feelings aside. They all wanted me to know that they would support me every step of the way.

The next person I had to tell was Vee. His reaction stunned me. When he found out that I was pregnant he immediately started talking about marriage. Despite the drama and trouble he was getting into in New York, Vee was prepared to move back to the city and build a family. We both knew our relationship was different. I wasn't sure that he was the person I wanted to build a life with. I didn't want Vee to be my husband. I wanted him to be my friend, but the pregnancy changed everything. Vee and I had made some adult decisions that could cost us our futures. We were both young and had no idea what kind of life was waiting for us as a result of our reckless behavior. I felt guilty and ashamed about the pregnancy and knew that my life was going to drastically change. Vee and I decided we would work things out and start the process of raising a child together.

The date was February 27, 1996. It felt good to be back in Queens. I was writing and recording lots of music. Vee and I were still living nearly nine hundred miles apart but we spoke every day and made plans to build our family. That morning I wasn't feeling well. I had passed a long night in the studio the night before. I had been feeling sharp pains in my stomach the night before but I blamed it on the White Castle food I was eating. I tried my best to ignore the pain even though it was still there in the morning. My first OB/GYN appointment was coming up in just a few days. I needed to find out how far along I was with the pregnancy and to get a better understanding of when my baby was going to enter the world. I figured that if I could just make it to that appointment I could find out why I wasn't feeling well and find out how my pregnancy was progressing.

About an hour later as I sat in bed listening to the morning show on HOT 97FM and trying my best to relax, I felt something running down my leg. I thought I was peeing on myself. I quickly sat up. My heart jumped when I realized that blood was running down my thighs. At first, I thought it was my menstrual cycle. Despite the fact that I was pregnant, I had been having my period. I figured my body was going through some abnormal changes. I tried my best to remain calm.

I decided to get up and take a shower. I recalled hearing that a woman could slow down her cycle by taking a hot shower, so I gave it a shot. It only took a few minutes to realize that I was not having a normal period. The bleeding didn't stop. It became heavier. I noticed large blood clots and grew worried. The sharp pains in my stomach became worse. I started to panic. I was crying uncontrollably. Something was terribly wrong. I had to do something.

Aunt Barbie was at work and my cousin, Cristal, wasn't home. My uncle, Carnel, was still sleeping but he didn't know what was going on with me. I was scared to tell him that I was pregnant so I kept it from him. I started feeling alone in the house and decided to call 911. I had no clue what was happening with my body. I started to get dressed and prepared to leave. The pain was getting worse with each passing moment. The ambulance arrived within minutes and I slipped out of the house before my uncle got up.

A few minutes later, I arrived at the medical center in Jamaica, Queens. The scene was more like a train station than a hospital. I felt extremely frightened because I was so young and alone. People were rushing in and out of the building. In the middle of the chaos, I was immediately admitted because I was pregnant and my fever was hovering around 102.

After a few minutes of sitting in the emergency room, I started to feel uncomfortable. There were so many staff members checking in on me but they seemed to be unprofessional. While they were attempting to check my vitals and draw blood, one of the nurses poked me incorrectly causing me to bleed. I started to grow aggravated. My nervousness became more acute when I noticed a lot of medical students and residents around. Finally, after what felt like an eternity in the emergency area, they moved me to another room where they did my examination.

That is when the doctors made a grim discovery. I had dilated and, as a result, would not be able to carry my pregnancy to term. I was devastated.

I still felt the physical pain but my mind seemed to go numb. A rush of emotions came over me and I cried uncontrollably. The nurses tried to console me but I was hurt, confused, and shamed.

"I'm so sorry that you will not be able to keep the baby," a nurse whispered to me, "but because of your blood loss and fever, it would be detrimental to try to keep the baby if you haven't already lost it."

I just cried. The nurse informed me of the next steps to avoid any further damage to my body. She told me that the doctors would have to perform a dilation and curettage. I had never heard of a D&C procedure before. She told me that they would have to clean my uterus wall and make sure I didn't have any infections. I agreed to get the procedure done. I was going to lose my first baby and there was nothing I could do about it.

I was beyond emotional. I called Aunt Barbie. She told me she would join me later at the hospital. Then, I called Vee. He was devastated by the news. He offered to fly up from Atlanta to come be with me but I told him that there was no need. The procedure would be quick and I would be released from the hospital the same day if everything went as planned. Before I went into surgery, I called my mother. I told her the sad news and she immediately shared my pain. I cried over my loss as she tried to console me.

"I just want you to know that I was never against this pregnancy," my mother said. "God knows best and he doesn't make mistakes."

I started to make peace with the terrible news. My mother's words gave me hope when I needed it the most. I was ready to go through with the procedure and move on with my life.

A few minutes later I went into surgery under heavy anesthesia. When I woke up, a few nurses were right in my face. They kept asking me how I felt. They were trying to gauge whether or not I was conscious enough to speak.

"Everything went well with the surgery," one nurse said. "The baby was fully removed and you were given Pitocin to make you contract so you may feel nauseous from the medicine and the anesthesia. Again, I'm sorry about your loss, but you're still young and you can always try again."

I didn't respond but I wanted to tell her that I wasn't *trying* to get pregnant this time. Her comment aggravated me. I was ready to leave the hospital but they told me I had to stay a while because my heart rate was still high and they didn't want my fever to spike again.

"So, how do you feel?" The nurse asked.

I told her that I was feeling sick and that I needed to vomit. She gave me a bowl and I puked a few times. My stomach was still hurting so they moved me to another room and monitored my vitals. I heard babies crying in the same ward and I started to feel a rush of guilt again. I feared that I would never get to experience the joy of holding a newborn baby in my arms. I felt regret.

An older woman in my room was recovering from a hysterectomy. The twisted irony of my situation made me feel like I was in hell. I cried again as my mind raced with negative thoughts.

A few minutes later, a doctor came into my room. He asked me about my pain levels and wanted to confirm that I understood everything about the surgery. I told him that I understood everything but that my stomach was still hurting. I informed him that it felt like I needed to use the bathroom really bad.

"If you are able to walk then, yes, you can get up and go to the bathroom," the doctor said. "If you need anything the nurses will assist you. And once we get everything back to normal including your temperature, you will be cleared to go home."

"Okay," I responded.

"Are you by yourself? Do you have a way to get home?" the doctor asked. "Who is going to come and get you?"

"I know my aunt is coming up here," I said, "so I will be leaving with her."

The doctor nodded his head and left the room. I eventually gathered the strength to get up and head to the bathroom. My body was weak and my stomach felt heavy. With each passing second my stomach hurt worse. I moved faster to get to the bathroom. It felt like I had to defecate. I stood over the toilet but nothing came out. All of a sudden a heard a huge gush and almost fainted at the sight of all the blood that was ejected from my body. I pulled the help-cord in a panic. I was too shocked to yell for help. A nurse rushed into the bathroom.

"Oh, my God!" the nurse unconsciously screamed.

A second nurse rushed in to assist. She took one look at the floor and almost panicked as well.

"Somebody get a container!" the first nurse yelled.

"For what?" A third nurse asked as she rushed in.

"There is a fully intact fetus on the floor!" the first nurse yelled.

I couldn't believe my ears. I just closed my eyes and felt all the blood rush from my head. I was ready to crawl in a corner and just die. The nurses scrambled to secure the bloody fetus off the floor. I immediately felt traumatized. The nurses helped me back to my bed and started working on me again. I couldn't believe what was happening to me. I started questioning my decisions and even started questioning God. It felt like he was punishing me for everything I had done leading up to that day.

My aunt arrived at the hospital not long after the incident. She stormed into my room with a look of fury in her eyes.

"What are they doing to you up here?" Aunt Barbie yelled.

Aunt Sheila and Uncle Peter came flying into the hospital, too. Everyone was upset. They couldn't understand how the hospital botched my surgery and almost caused more damage to my body. The doctors tried to make excuses and cover up their incompetence. One doctor asked me if I tried a home abortion citing that it may have been the reason for my high fever. They also tried to blame it on the possibility that I was having twins and that the other fetus was hiding. My uncle Peter didn't want to hear any excuses from the doctors. He told them that we would be hiring an attorney and seeking a malpractice lawsuit against the hospital.

It was hard for me to cope with the emotional trauma I experienced that day. For the next few weeks I cried continually. I kept asking God, "What did I do to deserve all of this?" The results came back from the hospital and I was informed that it was a sixteen-week-old male fetus. I had been pregnant with a son. The news hit me even harder.

Uncle Peter followed through with the lawsuit. When I was asked to answer questions at the disposition, the emotions of the botched miscarriage were fresh in my mind. My lawyers started to question my mental stability. After a while, I even started to ask myself if I was going crazy. I was instructed to admit myself to Bellevue hospital in New York for a psychological assessment. I agreed to visit Bellevue but later declined to continue once they asked me to take the medication from their doctors. The details surrounding my miscarriage caused me to distrust all doctors. I had heard of people that visited Bellevue hospital and came out even crazier than before they went inside. Not wanting to be the victim of any other incompetent doctors I decided to drop the entire lawsuit.

The pain of that cold February day was hard to shake. I was on an emotional rollercoaster. Finding out that I was pregnant by someone that I didn't want to marry and losing my child nearly shattered me. I carried a lot of fear with me for a long time. I even started to feel like someone or something was out to harm me. It took me nearly six years to get over that pain. It wasn't until the birth of my first child that I was able to fully put that day behind me and move on with my life. I eventually got a tattoo on my arm in remembrance of my lost son. I was a big fan of Robert De Niro at the time and I had been planning to name my son Denero. I got a tattoo of an infant boy boxing with the name Denero and the date 02-27-96 underneath.

When my youngest son sees the tattoo he always asks me who the boy boxing on my arm is. I tell my son that it's him when he was a baby. I haven't had the courage to tell him the truth. It has taken so long for the shame and the guilt of that day to lift. Now, I'm ready to share my story in hopes that it will help to heal someone else who has experienced a similar nightmare.

Vee and I eventually parted ways. Our fading relationship was all but over after we lost our child. For a while, I thought about Vee and how he was doing. I always wondered if he ever got over the miscarriage. My questions were answered a few years later when I ran into Vee on the set of one of my music videos. I was shocked to see him. We embraced like we hadn't seen each other in a million years. He was with his son. I felt so proud of him. Vee was finally a daddy. We talked for a while and he introduced me to his child.

"Say hi," Vee said to his son. "This was supposed to be your mommy."

The odd statement shocked me. I immediately thought about the calm words that came from my mother's mouth on that day back in 1996. Knowing that God doesn't make mistakes always put me at peace about our lost. I learned that only God knows his plan and sometimes we must accept his will. I had to realize that it wasn't the end of the world. God delivered me from that situation for a reason. I didn't die that day and there was more of me to give. These lessons I have learned are valued treasures.

*

Cynthia Loving

Chapter Ten

"*Think and believe you will be successful and it shall be so.*"

I heard that advice a lot when I was younger. Despite the personal drama I was experiencing, I tried to keep my mind focused on my dream to be an entertainer. I was still living in New York and my desire to be successful was stronger than ever. I needed a solid career as a backup plan, so I considered attending college in New York. Every attempt I made to apply to school was met with enormous resistance. I was under eighteen at the time and colleges would not accept my application without my parents' consent. I was living with my aunt at the time. The school registrar was acting funny about granting her power of attorney over my affairs. The university gave me a hard time about my paperwork and made it nearly impossible for me to apply. I was a scholar in high school and my transcript was flawless, but there was nothing I could present to the college that would change their minds. The process ultimately brought me to tears.

I eventually gave up the fight. I chalked it up as a sign that college was not in God's plan for me. I decided to attend hair school instead. I was good with my hands so I knew I could make decent money. Aunt Barbara, Uncle Carnel, and my cousin, Cristal, helped me pay for my classes. I worked in a hair salon in Queens to make ends meet while I continued to chase my dream.

One late evening in 1996, I woke up with an excruciating headache. The pain seemed to shoot from my head down to the middle of my spine. I got out of bed and headed down to my aunt's kitchen to get a drink of water. A strange feeling came over me. Something deep inside of me told me that someone in my family was in trouble. I immediately called my mother to check on her. After a few minutes on the phone I discovered that my intuition was eerily correct.

"Your brother, Tim, is in the hospital," my mother said. She tried to remain calm but I could tell that she was taking the news very hard. "We are not sure what happened to your brother. His friend, Sean, took him to the hospital."

My heart dropped to the floor. It was impossible for me to hold back my tears. The first reports we received was that my brother had been drinking and had fallen off the back of a truck. The news sounded strange to me. I had never known Tim to be so careless. After a few hours, the truth started to come to the surface. The news shocked us all.

Tim had been hanging out with Sean earlier that evening. They were celebrating the fact that Tim was moving to New York for good. My brother was planning to stay with his god-parents and to get a job in the big city. While they were hanging out, Tim noticed that a young woman being assaulted by a man. Tim was never the type of person to turn a blind eye to a female being violated. He rushed to the woman's aid and tried to break up the altercation. The man turned his anger onto my brother and hit him in the head with a baseball bat. The violent altercation was over quickly but the damage to my brother was permanent.

Later that evening, Tim tried to go home and put the scuffle behind him. Sean realized my brother was in bad shape and decided to take him to the hospital. Sean's decision saved my brother's life. Tim coded nearly fifteen times or more that evening. He was still a teenager but, as was explained to me, he had died for nearly every year that he had been alive. The assault had caused severe brain hemorrhaging. The doctors informed us that if Tim would have stayed home that evening he would have passed away in his sleep. The news was devastating to my family. We couldn't believe Tim had nearly died because he came to the aid of a total stranger. Tim was a protector and it seemed that the enemy was trying to end his life yet again. The doctors told us that Tim would have permanent brain damage. Although my brother suffered major injuries that evening he managed to battle back, but the trauma still affects Tim today. Neither my brother nor my family has ever fully recovered from the assault.

A few days later, I left New York and headed back to North Carolina. I wanted to be around my family while my brother was recovering. My aunt was leaving New York to move to Philadelphia. I would have to move out of my aunt's house. I needed a new plan. Watching how the pain and grief was consuming my family had a profound effect on me. It was time for me to go hard. My family needed to be straight. I decided to take on the responsibility to make something happen.

As fate would have it, I received a call from New York a short time later. I was told that R&B singer N'Dea Davenport had removed herself from The Jazzmatazz Tour with Hip-Hop artist Guru. There was a vacancy for a background singer and the job was mine if I could make it back to New York for the audition. At the time, I didn't have a dime to my name. I told my dad about the opportunity and, as always, he supported me completely. He drove me up to New York the next day and I auditioned for Guru. I sang my rendition of "His Eye Is on the Sparrow" in the middle of Guru's living room. He loved my sound and I got the job.

I was excited and relieved when I got the nod to head back out on tour. It was time for me to take my career seriously. I was still in my teens and had the amazing opportunity to travel the world with Guru and the Jazzmatazz Tour. I was meeting some great people and making a lot of connections. Things would only get better.

When we got off tour, I would hang out with Guru and record songs in D&D Studio in New York City. I met dozens of artists including Jeru the Damaga, Dame Dash, and even Jay-Z. Everyone was nice to me and looked at me as if I was the cool girl on the block. I saw see a number of girls being treated like trash by these same industry people but they never disrespected me. I still dressed like a tomboy and it seemed like a lot of people treated me like the little sister in the group. Everyone I met back then showed me love. My name started buzzing around the industry. I gradually started writing songs for different artists.

One day, Renee and I were having one of our many

discussions about the industry. I was looking for a production company to help me get my songs placed with the major record labels. Renee told me that she was working with a production company called Flava Hood out of Queens, New York. She said they were well connected in the industry and suggested that I give them a shot. I always trusted Renee's advice so I decided to contact them. Eventually, I signed a contract.

Flava Hood was signed under Mecca Don Records who was signed under Elektra Records. Flava Hood produced a lot of music for Adina Howard, Michael Speaks, and a few other artists. I began writing and referencing many songs and started getting placement with both Mecca Don and Elektra Records. I was excited about the opportunity to work with Flava Hood and getting my songs placed. After a few months of working without payment, the euphoria began to dissolve and my suspicions began to rise.

Although I had plenty of touring experience, I was young and naive to the music business. Before working with Flava Hood, I was clueless about the placement process. I was under the impression that once I finished turning in a song that I would receive compensation for my work. It seemed that I could never get a straight answer when I asked the production company for any money. They told me that they were waiting for Elektra Records to "cut the checks." I grew impatient with the process. I was far from financially stable at the time and I was ready to get paid for my work. I tried to be patient with the executives at Flava Hood as they continued to reach out to the brass at Elektra Records.

One day, while we were in the studio, the executives at Flava Hood were trying to reach out to Elektra Records.

We were all looking to get paid and the vibe in the room was tense. After a few minutes, I could tell that something was wrong. The executives at Flava Hood were not getting through to the A&R at Elektra Records. I couldn't take it anymore. My patience was wearing thin.

"You know what, just let me call!" I yelled out.

Everyone in the room was clearly taken aback by my idea. I got the phone number from one of the staff members and called up to Elektra's main offices. The A&R at the time was Merlin Bobb and his assistant was Rick Brown. I quickly dialed the number and waited for someone to answer. I was ready to find out why we were not getting paid.

"Elektra Records," Rick Brown answered the phone.

"Merlin Bobb's office, how may I help you?"

"Can I speak to Merlin?" I blurted.

"Who's calling?" Rick asked.

"Lil' Mo," I replied.

"Ummm, he's in a meeting right now," Rick quickly said. "What's this in regards to-"

"He's not in no meeting!" I raised my voice and cut Rick off. "I just seen Merlin walking in the hallway."

Rick was clearly stunned by my response. He paused for a moment and I could hear his wheels turning through the phone. I had never met Merlin Bobb and I had no clue what he looked like. I was in Queens at the time and was nowhere near the Elektra Record offices. I needed to take a gamble and get some answers from Merlin. I knew I was taking a risk but, at this point, I had nothing to lose. Rick Brown and I got into a heated argument. He would not allow me to speak to Merlin Bobb and I continued to curse him out.

"I'm the manager down here for Flava Hood," I shouted. "I'm trying to find out where our money is."

"Well, if you was some big ole' manager you would have known that you was supposed to get your first end check before anyone stepped inside the studio," Rick yelled at me.

A light bulb went off in my head. Before the conversation with Rick, I thought I was only to get paid after the songs were completed. I never realized that I needed to ask for a deposit or a down payment before I did any work in the music industry. Although Rick was yelling in my ear at the time, the information he relayed to me was invaluable.

The argument continued until Merlin Bobb finally came to the phone. I told Merlin that I was Lil' Mo. He realized that I was writing and referencing songs for his artists at Elektra. He asked me to come down to his office.

A few days later, I met with Merlin and Rick. I didn't know what to expect from this meeting, but I had prepared myself for the worse. When I walked into the Elektra Records offices, Merlin and Rick were shocked.

"Wait a minute?" Merlin laughed and looked at me. "You're so little and you was talking all that trash on the phone?"

Merlin, Rick, and I immediately hit it off. I apologized to Rick Brown about the argument and he understood my position. Merlin said my tenacity made an impression on him and said Elektra Records wanted to sign me to a record deal. Merlin told me that Sylvia Rhone wanted to meet me. I couldn't believe it.

"Yeah, right," I said. "Flava Hood has been producing for y'all for years and she never wants to meet with them, but she wants to meet with me?"

Despite my skepticism, Merlin Bobb was a man of his word. I eventually met with Sylvia Rhone. The meeting changed my life. I had heard Sylvia's name throughout the industry but I had never seen her. I was expecting to see a stuffy, out of touch, middle-aged woman sitting behind the desk, but Sylvia was down to earth and powerful. She took a chance on a young girl from Long Island and I'm forever grateful to her. Sylvia and I have remained friends over the years. I still call on her for career advice.

The thrill of signing my first deal with Elektra Records was something I could never describe in words. I didn't have a demo and I was barely experienced in the business. By keeping my mind on my goals and trusting the process, it seemed that everything I dreamed of was becoming a reality. What started out as a gamble spun in my favor. The results have been nothing short of a blessing from above.

*

Chapter Eleven

I was only in the music business for a short while before I learned the most valuable lesson of this industry. A major part of success in the entertainment world is not about what you know; it's all about *who* you know. I learned how to network and stay visible by watching a lot of people in the music industry. Things change very fast in the business and knowing the right people can make a world of difference. Through my connections, I was able to work with independent artists, Grammy-Award winners, and even a few musical legends.

Missy Elliot was very influential in my early career. When I was on tour with Missy, I met countless singers, rappers, and music executives. I worked hard to get next to these people and to maintain my relationships with them. My goal was always to work with the best people in the business, also to make them my friends. Missy Elliot was not only a very good friend but she was also a great mentor. She taught me many lessons about how to navigate the business. She also introduced me to a lot of people who helped my career.

One afternoon while we were in the studio, Missy informed me that Whitney Houston was coming to record a song. I was shocked and thrilled by the news. Ever since I was a young girl, I had looked up to Whitney Houston. Her powerful voice was a gift that every young girl aspired to have one day. When I learned that Whitney got her start in the church, I immediately identified with her story. She was a classy entertainer who made it acceptable for church women to sing secular music. When Missy Elliot told me that I would be working with the great Whitney Houston, I was speechless.

Missy asked me to record and reference a song for Whitney called "YES" before she arrived at the studio. I had never met Whitney before, so I didn't know what to expect. She was a superstar diva in her own right and a living legend. Whitney arrived at the studio and I couldn't believe how cool she was. She was down to earth and knowledgeable about the game. I felt like I was dreaming as I worked in the booth with Whitney. I fed the lyrics to her while she rehearsed and recorded her song. She was a joy to work with.

"Ooooo, girl, I just love your voice," Whitney complimented me. "You are from the church, aren't you? I love your voice."

Whitney pulled a Fishermen's Friend Throat Lozenge out of her pocket and handed me one and told me these were great for us "real singers." I laughed but was overjoyed to share the booth and a "singer's candy" with one of the greatest singers of our time.

I smiled at the sincerity of Whitney's compliment. I was just a young artist getting my feet wet in the industry and her words gave me a much needed boost of confidence. Whitney and I immediately hit it off. I have met a lot of people in the industry but working with Whitney Houston was an experience that I will never forget.

When I got off tour with Missy Elliot, I started working harder than ever. I focused hard on my goals and it seemed that I was being contacted daily for more work. I sacrificed a lot to keep my momentum going. I never wanted to lose my position in the business so I did everything I could to keep my name buzzing. I was moving fast and really didn't have much else on my mind. I didn't realize how much I was sacrificing until I got a phone call from my mother about my younger sister, Charese.

"I have good news about your sister," my mother said.

"Charese is not getting into any more fights. The cops awarded her a certificate for not fighting for the past thirty days. She is back on the straight and narrow."

Despite the joy in my mother's voice, the news was an instant reality check for me. I had been worried about my baby sister. Things with my family had changed drastically since I moved to New York to chase my career. My younger sister had been getting into a lot of trouble, fighting, stealing, and raising hell constantly. I had been receiving calls about Charese a few times a month. My sister even had joined a gang. No one had a clue as to why my sister was changing so drastically. Despite growing up in a great household, my sister was becoming a wild baby, part 2.

A few years after I attended E.E. Smith High School, it was Charese's turn to navigate those same hallways. By the time my sister started her freshman year, the school had changed for the worse. E.E. Smith had become even more dangerous than when I attended. Charese stayed in trouble. She started acting out and running with a bad element. I couldn't help but blame myself for her behavior.

Just before I graduated from high school, I was

preparing to move away to New York. My plan was to put North Carolina in the rearview mirror and never look back. As my career started to take off, I called home less often. At one point, I stopped communicating with everyone. It never was my intention to cut my family completely off, but I allowed my rigorous schedule to interfere. I rarely called to check in on my sister. I wasn't there to guide Charese or to advise her how to survive as a teen in Fayetteville. My sister didn't have anyone she could talk to.

One day while Charese was at school, she was injured badly. Her fingers had gotten caught in the steel doors in one of the hallways. She was rushed to the hospital. It was a miracle that her finger was not severed. It was clear that Charese was upset with me when I talked to Charese about the incident.

"See! If you was here to be my big sister, none of this would have happened," Charese said.

My baby sister's words stuck with me. I knew I had to play a more active role in her life. It hurt me to see Charese going through so much as a teen without me there to guide her. I decided that when I finally signed my deal and became financially stable I would make some major changes. I wanted to fill the empty space that I allowed to grow in the middle of our relationship. As fate would have it, the military reassigned my father. He moved the family to Fort Meade, Maryland. It seemed that Maryland would be the last stop on the *Loving Train*. My father suggested that I buy a home in the area, so I took his advice. I still had my apartment in New York. This way, I would have a home closer to my family. To everyone's delight, Charese eventually graduated high school. She moved in with me and we became even closer than we had been before I left.

One day, I got a call from Missy Elliot's management company. They informed me that Missy needed me to perform with her on Jay Leno's show. The management company asked me to put together a small group of background singers for the show. It was perfect timing. Charese had a great singing voice, so I added her to the group of background vocalists. Along with my good friend Mary, we headed to Los Angeles to rehearse. Later, we performed live with Missy Elliot. Having my sister with me was amazing. My parents always taught us to look out for one another and watching my sister shine on television was a proud moment for me.

Over the years, Charese has become very active in my career, from going on tour with me to being my personal hair stylist to even helping me run my music label. My sister and I have a bond that can never be broken. When I was younger, I did not realize how my absence was affecting my sister and the choices she made.

When Charese and I reminisce about her teen years, I am shocked by everything she has been through. Charese has survived treacherous attacks at the hands of rival kids from other schools. She has been detained multiple times for fighting and running with a wild group of kids. One day, I learned Charese had experienced more pain than I ever had imagined.

While having a discussion one day, what we like to call "bro talk," Charese revealed to me that she had been raped when she was in high school. She told me that she skipped classes one day and went with her friends to a skip-party. A boy she had known from school had taken advantage of my sister. The disgusting details of the rape crushed me. I cried with Charese and I cried for Charese. She told me that for the longest time she didn't tell anyone from the family about the sexual assault. She was left to deal with the pain alone.

Nothing hurt me more than hearing that my baby sister had been raped. It tore my heart to shreds. I was devastated. I blamed myself for not being there to tell the rapist he would DIE if he ever hurt my little sister again. I had failed Charese. I had failed my family.

I have always felt compelled to apologize to Charese for not being there for her. I was so focused on my own desire for success that I didn't realize Charese was crying out for help. I had abandoned her when she was a teen. I promised never to abandon her again. Her strength is amazing and she never hesitates to look out for my best interest. She will protect her big sister in a heartbeat and never will let anyone get one over on me.

Even with all the pain she has endured, Charese has always remained her naturally loving self. My sister has mentored troubled teens to give them a ray of hope. She has helped young girls who have suffered from physical abuse, child neglect, drug addiction, and sexual assault. Charese knows that her life could have travelled down the same destructive path, so she does what she can to make a difference. While some people look up to strangers, Charese is my hero. Leaving my family behind to pursue my dreams almost cost me my sister. Now that we are tighter than ever, nothing will separate us ever again.

Chapter Twelve

Signing my first record deal was a dream come true. The year was 1999 and it seemed like the world around me was changing quickly. The hot topic that year was Y2K and the coming of the new millennium. Everyone was on high alert and there was a nervous energy in the air. People everywhere seemed to be moving fast and preparing themselves for something big. I was hustling for a different purpose. I was excited to get a six-figure deal from a major record company. My life was on fast forward. I was going harder than ever to keep up with everything and everyone. I continued to write and record songs. I chased my passion.

Not long after getting my record deal, Elektra Records scheduled promotional shows to hype the forthcoming album. With every show, my circle of industry friends grew. It was a crazy time in the music business. We all had one common trait back then. We were all "up" – staying up, turning up, tearing up, drinking up, eating up, blazing up, and even dating up.

I was single at the time and living in between New York and Maryland. Although industry people surrounded me, I couldn't help but feel alone. When work was done and the music stopped, I wanted to live my life and have fun and I didn't want to be by myself. Just the thought of strange men trying to holler at me when I was in public always made me leery about traveling alone. A boyfriend was the furthest thing from my mind but I wanted someone in my life to shake the lonely rut I was in.

    I found myself recording a lot of music as the New Year rushed in. I released a song called "Ta Da" and my diehard fans loved it. The record label had been expecting a larger response from the song so they kept me on the road to promote. I was going from venue to venue gaining momentum for the upcoming album.

    One evening, while I was wrapping up a promotional show, a young rapper out of New Jersey approached me. He was a hype-man for a gospel rapper that performed earlier that evening. I could tell by the slick look on his face that this dude was not looking to discuss music with me. He introduced himself as one thing, but I liked to call him F.A.M.M. (Fake Ass M&M). He dressed like the typical rapper, baggy jeans, a fly hip-hop shirt, and a doo rag on his head. He was extremely polite when he approached me but I could tell that he had an edge. I always had a thing for guys that were rough around the edges. He certainly fit the mode, but there was something else about him that immediately fascinated me. F.A.M.M. had swag. He was cute. And he was white.

    Before F.A.M.M., I had never dated a white guy – ever. However, after my music career began to take off, I started to entertain the thought of dating outside of my race. Because I was such a tomboy and hung around men all the time, I would hear them talking about white women. I remember hearing black guys joke about how they were going to date white women when they became successful. They always said that white women would do anything for them. Hearing statements like that only made me more curious about white men. Now, my music career was taking off and reaching new heights. It seemed as if F.A.M.M. had come into my life at just the right "curious" time.

In the beginning, F.A.M.M. and I hit it off well. He was the coolest white boy that I had ever met. The way he spoke and the way he dressed reminded me of Eminem. F.A.M.M. and I started hanging out and we became closer every day. When we were together, F.A.M.M. was cordial and considerate, a true gentleman. He opened doors for me and helped me out whenever he could. I liked that about him.

F.A.M.M. grew up in a rough hood in New Jersey. F.A.M.M. never missed an opportunity to show off his slang. He even used the word *nigger* without hesitation. I never felt insulted or embarrassed by him. I always joked that F.A.M.M. didn't think he was a white guy. He thought he was a light-skinned black man. Everybody thought he was cool so I didn't have a problem building a relationship with him. After a few months of dating we eventually became a semi-couple. I officially had my token white boy on my arm.

A few months later, I moved out of my apartment in New York and moved back into my house in Maryland. F.A.M.M. was waiting on a job in the area. He asked if he could stay with me until he moved into his new place. I agreed. I enjoyed being around him and we had a lot of fun together. F.A.M.M. even went to church with my family on a few occasions. He would keep the house clean and all that, but after a while our relationship began to take a turn. We had been going strong for a few months without any problems. That would all change the day I received a message shook my trust in him.

    I was still sleeping early one morning when my cousin Celeste paged me. The sun had barely risen so I knew something wasn't right. My cousin Celeste was a godsend for me. She was like my *Olivia Pope,* from the television drama series *Scandal.* Celeste would monitor my fan pages and my social media sites and make sure nothing was damaging or threatening the Lil' Mo brand. Before Facebook, Twitter and Instagram came on the scene, we used The Official Lil' Mo Myspace Page to stay connected with my fans. While monitoring my MySpace page, my cousin Celeste noticed that one of my followers was posting negative comments about me.

    "Hey, Mo, is somebody playing on your page?" Celeste texted.

    "I'm not sure," I responded. "What's going on?"
"There is some girl posting negative comments about you on your MySpace page," Celeste said.
"She is calling you a home wrecker and saying that you are breaking up a happy home."

    The news shocked me. I jumped out of bed and went straight to my computer. I logged onto my page and took a look at the messages. I was floored to see multiple comments bashing my current relationship and me. I was irate. I printed out the comments and studied the accusations. I confronted F.A.M.M. and asked him about the girl. His response hit me like a bombshell.

    When we first started dating, F.A.M.M. told me that

he had a child and that he and his baby's mother had broken up. After she started posting comments on my page, F.A.M.M. finally confessed to me that they were married but had since separated. He said that she was holding up their divorce. I was beyond pissed off. I couldn't believe that he had lied to me.

F.A.M.M. tried to explain himself. He told me that he was scared to reveal the truth. I couldn't understand how he could form his lips to lie to me but he couldn't form his lips to tell me the truth. His confession made me lose all trust in him. He had committed the ultimate sin. I always have hated liars. People have done plenty of wrongs things to me in my life, but once they lie to me I have no choice but to cut them off no matter the circumstance. By lying to me, F.A.M.M. had written himself out of my life.

F.A.M.M. called his younger sister. F.A.M.M.'s sister had sided with his baby's mother and also was posting negative comments on my page. F.A.M.M. confronted his sister and told her to remove the comments. I was threatening to sue everyone involved. The last thing I needed was my name being dragged through the home-wrecking mud. I worried that if the label got wind of this drama then this could become a bigger problem. F.A.M.M.'s sister and his baby's mother eventually removed the negative messages but the damage was done. It would be just a matter of time before F.A.M.M. and I would go our separate ways.

About a week later I was back on the road. The record label scheduled me for more promotional dates so I headed back out to pump the album. F.A.M.M. was still living in my home in Maryland. Even though I knew our relationship was fading I didn't see a problem with helping him out. His job was starting soon so he would eventually have his own place. One afternoon my sister, Charese, called me when I was out on the road. She was also staying at my house with her young son, Brey'n. The angst in my sister's voice immediately concerned me. She told me that my nephew had been acting up and that F.A.M.M. had yelled at him. I couldn't believe what Charese was telling me. Brey'n was not only my nephew but he was also my godson. I didn't have any kids at the time and I always treated Brey'n as if he was my own. A vision of F.A.M.M. chastising my godson flashed in my mind. I became hot. My father always taught us to protect each other. He always preached family first. Anger boiled inside me. F.A.M.M. was clearly out of line. My anger reached another level when I thought about this grown white man yelling at a young black child. I started to question if the scolding was racially charged. I almost felt like a freedom fighter rising up against Jim Crow. I no longer looked at F.A.M.M. as a friend. It was time to check him. Charese put F.A.M.M. on the phone and I yelled at him.

"When I get home, we need to talk." I shouted.

A few days later I was back in Maryland. I was still upset at F.A.M.M. and couldn't wait to confront him about my nephew Brey'n. When I got back to my house, F.A.M.M. was there. I remember yelling at him the moment we saw each other.

"Bitch, if you ever yell at my motherfuckin' nephew, in your motherfuckin' life again, I will kill you!" I shouted.

F.A.M.M. tried to explain the situation. I didn't let him get a word in. I was furious. I was holding a heavy metal candlestick in my hand and I pointed it directly at his face.

"Brey'n is not your child and you are not his uncle," I

yelled.

F.A.M.M. tried to cut me off and started raising his voice. The confrontation grew more heated.

"Don't play with me," I shouted. "That is not your place to try to discipline my nephew. You don't do that. If you yell at my motherfuckin' nephew again, Bitch, I will knock you out of that motherfuckin' window."

F.A.M.M. recognized my rage and didn't say another word. I was in full beast mode and ready to do anything to protect my family. I told F.A.M.M. to leave my house. The lies about his marital status were still festering in my mind. This current situation was the tipping point. I needed F.A.M.M. to remove himself from my life, physically and emotionally. He was not invited around my family again. When he left my house that day, I would not reach out to him again. We parted ways, for good.

A few years went by and I eventually received a message from F.A.M.M.'s ex-wife. She found me through one of my social media sites and said she needed to speak to me. Her message was remorseful and contrite. She stated that she couldn't move on with her life until she apologized to me. She informed me that she was hurt about F.A.M.M. being with me but also said that he was living a lie. We conversed for a while to clear the air. Being a Christian woman, I had to forgive her. As fate would have it, we became good friends. F.A.M.M.'s ex-wife came out to my shows and brought her kids along. We have no ill feelings toward each other. Her children love me and we are all friends to this day.

The brief relationship I had with F.A.M.M. taught me a lot about people. F.A.M.M. was not a bad guy and I really enjoyed our time together. However, his lies put me in an inexcusable situation. He knew my religious beliefs and I knew his beliefs as well. The last thing I wanted on my conscience was to be involved with a married man. I thank God that F.A.M.M.'s secret came to the light and that I was protected from any impending backlash. F.A.M.M. was not upfront with me. That eventually destroyed our relationship. He tried to justify his lies by saying he was afraid of losing me. It was his fear that hurt me the most. I realized that F.A.M.M. was scared to lose Lil' Mo. He met Lil' Mo and that is the person he wanted to be with. He showed me that he would do anything to be with Lil' Mo, even deceive me. F.A.M.M. never cared about my compassionate and loving side. He didn't care enough about Cynthia to tell me the truth. In the end, his lies and deception caused him to lose both of us.

*

Chapter Thirteen

Da da da da.... da da da da da da da da...

The annoying music banged loudly in my ears. I nodded wildly to the beat and tried my best to conjure up a melody. The raw sound was crazy to me but I was confident I could make a hit record out of it. The engineer ran the track again. My manager waited quietly in the studio while I tried to work my magic. I started to grow frustrated. Nothing was coming to me. I took a quick glance at the clock on the wall and shook my head. I was running out of time. My window of opportunity was slowly slipping away. I was given just two hours to write, record, and finalize the song that I knew would save my career.

It was the fall of 2000 and I was ready to release my debut album. The executives at Elektra Records, my music label at the time, had approved most of the songs that we turned in, but they were not ready to give me a solid release date. Not only was I working on my album, but I was also writing and recording a lot of songs for different big-name artists. I was doing music with BlackStreet, Bow Wow, Angie Martinez, Jaheim, Tyrese, Keith Sweat, and even the late, great Gerald Levert. Nobody could tell me that I wasn't the shit. I was also coming off of the international success of two huge records. After writing and performing on Ja Rule's "Put It on Me" and Missy Elliot's "Hot Boyz," my career catapulted to a new level. Those songs were still banging on the radio and fresh in the minds of my fans. Despite the success of those records, I was ready to step out on my own and push my solo music into the marketplace.

    I was still signed to the production company, Flava Hood. We were working hard creating great music together. For almost a year, Elektra continued to push my album back. They blamed it on the lack of a radio hit. My previous singles "If You Want to Dance" (produced by Flava Hood) and "Ta Da" (produced by Anthony "Shep" Crawford) sold over 200,000 copies combined. The songs started to make noise on the radio but they never reached the crossover level. After two unsuccessful tries, the label was still pushing me to come up with a single that would bang to the masses.

    I started to grow frustrated with Elektra. Before I got signed, I thought the process of dropping an album would be simple. I thought I could record as many songs as I wanted and then choose which songs could be singles and pushed to the radio, but that wasn't the case. I soon found out that the A&Rs at the label were in charge of choosing the records. The A&Rs also work with the marketing and promotions department to get the song to the radio. One executive pulled me to the side and said, "Mo, your songs have to make it to the crossover market. It don't matter that a lot of people think you are hot around the way. You have to think outside of your region."

    After turning in a few more songs without the label

biting on any of them, I knew I would have to think outside the box and do something drastic. A lot of people started to get into my ear trying steer me away from Flava Hood. The production company was known for making hot music and I never complained about the results, but Flava Hood was not as connected to the radio stations as I needed them to be.

I learned about the power of connections in the music industry early in my career. I had seen a boatload of talented artists come and go whose careers were quickly cut short because they lacked a strong radio presence. I didn't want that to happen to me. I continued to work with Flava Hood but I needed to work with other producers to give me a different sound.

I turned to Jay Brown, one of the A&Rs at Elektra Records. He was my point of contact with the label but he was also an amazing friend. He worked with a number of big companies and also did publishing deals back then. Jay Brown believed in me from the second we met. He had heard my name and my music buzzing around the industry and he started pointing me in the right direction. He helped me get placement for more songs and introduced me to some great contacts. I had met a lot of people in the industry before I met Jay Brown, but because of his influence, Jay would re-introduce me to those same people and make them pay attention. I remember the day he introduced me to Jay-Z. I was already a fan of Jigga's music so it was cool to hear him say that he had heard my voice around. Jay-Z loved my sound. That's how I got on the "Parking Lot Pimpin'" song.

Jay Brown never hesitated to keep me on top of my business. He made sure that I wasn't out of sight and out of mind. He continued to introduce me to different people who helped my career prosper. He eventually pointed me in the direction of Loreal Coppedge.

I met Loreal on the set of my "Ta Da" video. We immediately hit it off and Loreal became my manager. She knew I was looking for a new sound and needed some new music to push to the label. She told me she was managing a lot of engineers and I remember being one of her first singers.

Loreal was also managing an engineer and producer by the name of Duro from Dessert Storm Records. Duro had won a Grammy Award for the work he did for Jay-Z on the "Hard Knock Life" album. His partner, DJ Clue, and he were big in the industry and had a direct link to the biggest radio station in the game, Hot 97FM in New York City. DJ Clue was also known for his "Cluemanatti" mixed tapes that created a platform for artists to gain more fans on the street level. I did work for Duro and DJ Clue in the past and it was good to reconnect with them through Loreal.

We all started working together and I asked DJ Clue if I could do a song for his mixed tape. He agreed without hesitation. He wanted me to do the intro for an album he was releasing called "The Professional 2." I agreed to do the song on one condition.

"Listen, Clue, you don't have to pay me but, in return, I need a song for my album," I said.

DJ Clue agreed to the deal. That small decision would change my life. A few weeks later, we were working at a studio in Los Angeles. I was recording a song for him and R&B artist, Canela Cox. After her session was over, I approached DJ Clue about the deal we previously discussed. I told him I was still searching for a single I could push to the radio. He let me hear some beats he was working on. At first, none of the music grabbed my attention. I continued listening while he was flipping through the tracks. Most of the songs were too R&B'ish. I was looking for a harder sound. I was looking for something that would bang in the streets and on the radio. Then I heard it.

Da da da da…. da da da da da da da da…

"Yo, what the hell is that?" I yelled, half annoyed and half excited. The track sounded so irritating, but the irritating beats were the ones that people remembered.

"This is a song I'm doing for M.O.P.," DJ Clue responded.

M.O.P. was a rugged hip-hop group out of Brooklyn. They were the true definition of street hip-hop. Their big song was "How About Some Hardcore" which was a hip-hop anthem in the early 90s.

"M.O.P.?" I blurted, "That doesn't even sound like a track that would be on their album."

DJ Clue laughed as we continued to listen to the track. He turned the volume up and let the music rock. It didn't have any other sounds to it just the harsh but addictive cadence. I nodded my head to it and felt the connection. I had to have this beat.

"Clue, listen. I know you gotta leave out of here and get back to New York but I need this track."

DJ Clue could see I was hyped about his music and agreed to give me a shot.

"Mo, there is only two hours left on this session," DJ Clue said, "so, if you could come up with a song and record it before the session is over then we can talk. I have to get back to New York to do my show on HOT 97 so you gotta get the track to me before the morning."

DJ Clue didn't have to tell me twice. The engineer loaded the music and Clue left the studio. I had less than two hours to make this happen. Things were a lot different back then. It was rare for artists to send MP3 files through the email. People wanted their music sent on an overnight flight to make sure they got the highest quality file. Most of the studios would make sure the music was on the last flight out of California so the label could get it on the east coast the next day. I knew I would have to "Delta Dash" the track from Los Angeles in order for DJ Clue to get it by the next day in New York.

I stepped into the booth and started the all too familiar journey of recording a song. This would be difficult. I was writing so much good music for other people that couldn't understand why I was drawing such a blank when it came to my own songs.

DJ Clue's beat started playing in my ears again. I nodded my head and played around with a few melodies. My mind was racing out of control, but so was the time.

"Oh, my God, why can't I come up with nothing?" I said to myself.

I was thinking too hard. I was feeling the pressure. Then, an idea hit me. I knew what I needed to relax myself and get into a creative mode.

Living in California came with a lot of perks, good sun, good money and, of course, good weed. Having marijuana available in a studio in Los Angeles was just as common as having bottled water available. People stopped by the studio all the time to supply the artists and engineers with whatever they needed. That particular night I didn't need a supplier. I kept a stash of marijuana on me for nights like this. I didn't have another minute to waste so I lit the blunt and took a long hard pull to the head. The natural taste of the weed started to calm me. A thick, white cloud filled the booth and before long I was officially taking flight. I was high as hell. I called it the "Snoop Dogg High."

I took another hard pull on the drug. My mind started to open up. My thoughts elevated beyond the clouds and I was ready. The engineer played the beat again in the headphones and I nodded. There was no time to write the song so I would have to freestyle it. The beat started to get louder and I began to feel more confident. I heard a melody come to my imagination and I started to vibe to the track.

Baby...they can't...play you... 'cause I'll...save you...with my...super...powers...

I felt a chill hit me. I don't know if it was the weed or the melody starting to consume me. This was it. The song sounded crazy from the moment I started the first riff. My creativity was back. The lid was officially blown off. I free styled the hook and the verses. To my surprise I came up with the entire song before the session ended. I was inspired by another song I tried to release called "Superwoman" but that song didn't get a lot of support from the label. I knew the song that I created tonight would be a hit. I decided to call it "Superwoman Pt. II." At that time, I had no clue just how big the record would become.

When DJ Clue heard the song the next day, he loved it. Flava Hood stepped in and helped to complete the song by adding the R&B touch to it. DJ Clue tested the first version on HOT 97. People loved it. Clue didn't wait for permission from Elektra Records to play a few pieces of the song. His logic was to test the record and let the label and the other radio stations catch up to him, but there was still something missing from the track.

A few days later, DJ Clue and I discussed the direction of the song. We both agreed that the song needed a hip-hop feel to it. We needed somebody to spit a verse on the track.

"Mo, you already worked with Ja Rule and Jay-Z," DJ Clue said. "You can get one of them on the record and I know that Elektra will cut the check."

I thought for a moment before I answered him. I knew Ja and Jay-Z had big names in the game at that time but I felt the song needed a different sound to it, something fresh and new.

"Nah, we don't need them," I said. "How about that dude that spells his name on your mixed tapes?"

"Who? Fab?" DJ Clue responded. "I can definitely get Fabolous."

"Are you serious?" I responded. I was clearly excited. I had heard Fabolous' verses on a number of DJ Clue's mixed tapes. I loved his flow.

"Oh, yeah, I'm goin' to call him right now," DJ Clue said.

Fabolous agreed to do the song and DJ Clue made sure he got the track. We were pressed for time so Clue told Fabolous that we needed the song back in a couple of days. Fabolous had it done the next day. DJ Clue set up the studio session and it was time to complete the record.

Loreal and I got to the studio before Fabolous and his manager. I felt anxious to meet him because I had heard his music for a few years but I had never seen him.

When Fabolous arrived at the studio, I was shocked. In walked this tall and lanky boy with a chipped-tooth smile, rocking a yellow bandana wrapped around his head. His fresh face made him seem younger than he really was. I was expecting some crazy looking, thugged-out dude from Brooklyn. Fabolous was laid back and focused. We immediately clicked. I joked around with his manager, Webb, while Fabolous prepared himself to lay down his vocals.

"So, you ready to do your rap?" I turned to Fabolous and smiled.

"No doubt," Fabolous nodded.

"So, what did you write down?" I asked.

"Nothing," Fabolous said, "I got it in my two-way."

He pulled out his Skytel Motorola P935. I was impressed that he wrote his songs on his pager. I remembered a key piece of advice I learned from Missy Elliot. She told me to leave the room when somebody was doing their part of a song so they won't feel embarrassed or subconscious about the session. Loreal, Webb, and I left the room and let Fabolous do his thing.

A few minutes later Duro, who was the engineer on the session, told us the song was done. I couldn't believe how fast they had laid the vocals and done a rough mix of the song.

"I hope you don't mind. I did a part on the intro," Fabolous said, "and I also did a verse in the middle of the song."

Before I could respond, Duro played the record. As soon as the beat dropped Fabolous' voice commanded everybody's attention.

I guess I ain't got no reason to mingle 'round...I found a superwoman that can leap from the truck in a single bound...

"Oh, my God!" I couldn't hide my excitement. The verse was fire and just what the song needed. I knew that the record was better than anything that I had submitted to Elektra. Everyone in the studio was vibing to the track. About two minutes into the song, the breakdown came. Fabolous' voice came back on the record.

Yo, the superwoman might've saved my day…Them skeeos I would've gave some play…Now I wouldn't even wave they way…

The song was getting better with each line. Fabolous was killing the record and then the magic happened. Just when I thought the song couldn't get better, he said it.

Da da da da…. da da da da da da DAMN!

When I heard that, I just screamed. I knew it was going to be a hit record. I looked to Fabolous who seemed to be amused by my reaction.

"Yo, when is your birthday?" I shouted over the music.

"November 18th," he answered.

"Wow, mine is November 19th!" I yelled again.

I knew we had a divine connection. We have been damned near brother and sister since that day. He was such a godsend for my project and for me. My budget was exhausted. I didn't have a lot of money to pay him, but that didn't matter. He told me he was just grateful for the opportunity to be on the track and his humility has always stuck with me. We ended up touring together and "Superwoman Part II" became successful well beyond my wildest dreams. It's amazing how many people still love the song today and how much energy is still behind the record when we perform it across the world.

I learned from that experience that the perfect record is not something you can plan. A perfect record has to feel right. I learned I couldn't put somebody on my song just because they were hot at the moment. The perfect record is about chemistry, being obedient and being ready. Because of his gratitude and his obedience, Fabolous' career has flourished.

I couldn't thank him enough for his contribution to my project if we both had a million years on this earth. If the pieces hadn't fallen into place to make that song happen, it's very possible that Elektra would have shelved me forever cutting my career short. It was a blessing from the heavens that I dropped a song called "Superwoman" to save my career. Soon I would have to become "The Woman of Steel" to prepare me for the traumatic change that was coming to my life.

Cynthia Loving

THE "LOVING" FAMILY

Photo Credit: Jacob D. Loving

Born at SouthSide Hospital
in Bayshore, NY

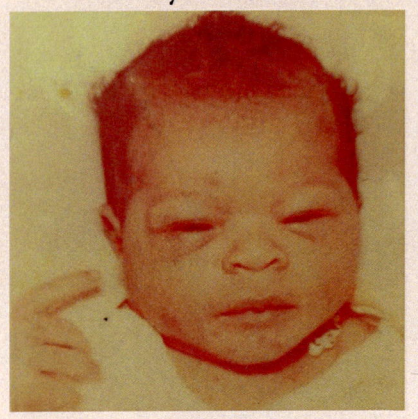

Little Cindy

Little Cindy

The "Loving" Children
Cynthia, Tim,
Charese and James

Photo Credit: Jacob D. Loving

Early Days with John P. Kee

High School Photo

Family Photo (Submitted by Anissa L Stewart)

Me With My "Superwoman Braids"

Me & Fabolous

Gold & Platinum Albums
(Photo Credit: Karl S. Dargan)

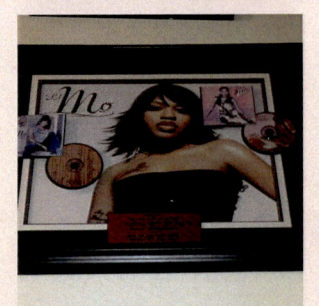

Selfie With Tyler Perry & Dynamite

Selfie With Benard Hopkins & Dynamite

Me, Fabolous & Dynamite

Me, 50 Cent & Dynamite

Me and Ty Dolla$

Me and Lil Boosie

Momma Diddy and Diddy

Me and Momma Diddy

On The Video Set With Dynamite
("Best Best Believe It")

Selfie With Aunt Shelia
(She Taught Me How To Sing)

Mother-In-Law Carla Dargan, Dynamite and I

Dargan Family Fun Day

Family Day

Family in Bed
Photo Credit: Mike Mike

Me and Michel'le On The Set of R&B Divas: LA

Me On The Set of R&B Divas: LA

Chapter Fourteen

In March of 2001, Elektra Records released "Superwoman Part II." The song already was buzzing in the clubs and all over the Hip-Hop and R&B radio stations. Not long after it was released, the song started sticking to the charts like a magnet. When the song cracked the Billboard Top 40, things really took off. The record label finally announced a release date for my debut album. The big day was June 26, 2001. I was anxious to drop "Based on a True Story" and officially launch my career as an R&B songstress.

Leading up to the release date, Elektra Records scheduled me for a number of appearances. They needed me to hype the album and I was more than happy to do so. I toured the nation doing radio and promotional events to get my fans excited about the big release. One of my last stops before my album dropped was in San Francisco. I was scheduled to perform at an event hosted by the radio station KMEL. It was slated to be a huge event. I was to share the stage with some of the hottest names in the industry at that time including, Case, Genuine, Tamia and Erick Sermon.

This was not the first time I was in the Bay Area. I had performed on the West Coast with a number of acts but never as a solo artist. I wanted to treat this event as my coming out party. It seemed as if the stars were aligning for me and I was ready to bring down the house.

    I arrived in San Francisco during the early part of that Friday morning. A strange feeling came over me the minute we touched down at the airport. Something wasn't right but I ignored my intuition as we made our way to the radio station. Even as I took to the airways to pump up the concert, I was feeling uneasy. Whenever I get one of those bizarre feelings in my gut I would always call my dad. I wanted him to pray for me. Unfortunately, I couldn't get a hold of him. I should have taken that as a sign to be more aware of my surroundings. I was so caught up in the hype of promoting my album that I never considered my safety to be an issue.

I ignored my feelings and went about the job of pushing this event. People around the Bay Area were hyped and ready to party. The day quickly turned into night and it was time for me to get ready for my performance.

    Before we left for the show, I made sure that my outfit was tight, in true Lil' Mo fashion. I decided to wear my slick denim skirt topped with a wife-beater. My signature braids were piped out in red, black and white that night. I wore them long and made sure they draped over my denim jacket. My outfit wasn't complete until I slipped into my Dolce & Gabbana heels. The American flag inspired shoes were a gift from celebrity stylist Misa Hylton. I loved when Misa styled me because she would always find exclusive pieces to make my outfits pop. When I looked down at those gorgeous shoes that night, I knew I was ready for a great show.

As we made our way to the sold out concert at The Warfield Theater I tried to stay focused on my performance. I was traveling with my boyfriend, AL, my road manager, Markey-Dew, and two of my backup dancers. I knew this trip was going to be a quick turnaround so we decided to travel light. My team was small. The only thing that was missing was security.

With the success of my latest single, I knew that my set was going to be a hit. I hit the stage to a thunderous reception. My back-to-back hits were banging loud and the energy in the building was insane. I felt unstoppable. I closed my show with the hit song everybody came to hear. "Superwoman" blared through the speakers. A huge smile came to my face when I heard everyone in the theater singing along with the record. The feeling was amazing. I was ready to ride this momentum all the way up to my album release that was just three days away.

After the show was over, my adrenaline was still sky high. Markey-Dew was pressed for time and needed to leave early to make it back to the airport. Markey-Dew was my eyes and ears whenever we were on the road. He would make sure we made it in and out of all venues safely and without any problems. When Markey-Dew left, I knew it was time to leave. I was now with my boyfriend Gus and my two backup dancers. We decided to make it an early night.

We left The Warfield Theater a little after 11pm. The parking lot was packed with people trying to get pictures and autographs from the celebrities as they left the venue. As we rushed to our limousine we noticed a small crowd starting to form near the vehicle. I was just about to get inside the backseat when I heard someone scream my name.

"Lil Mo...!"

I instinctively turned around. A large man approached. He was coming straight for me and no one reacted to him. He had a strange look on his face and cursed at me. He maliciously raised his fist and smashed me over the head with a champagne bottle. The violent impact sent everyone into a panic. My legs buckled from the crippling blow. I felt the bottom of my heel break and I crumbled to the asphalt.

"My shoe!" I yelled out. "Oh, my God...my shoe!"

I felt the champagne dripping from my head and tried to clear my eyes. I searched around for the heel of my Dolce & Gabbana limited edition shoe. I loved those shoes and hated the fact that the heel had broken. The harsh reality had escaped me. I was unconscious on my feet and never realized I had sustained a blow that nearly cost me my life. What I though was champagne dripping all over my face was actually blood from a huge gash on my head.

My ears started ringing and my eyes got blurry. The grim reality started to seep in along with the pain. My dancers were crying uncontrollably as they threw me into the backseat of the limo. The driver tore out of the parking lot and rushed to the nearest hospital.

"Why are y'all crying? Do y'all see my shoe? Where is Gus? Is he okay? Can somebody get my dad on the phone? Do y'all see my shoe!?"

My mouth was running a mile a minute but I was making no sense at all. I was clearly suffering from shock. My team tried to stop the bleeding but my head was leaking badly. I was in trouble.

"Tilt your head back, Mo!" one of the dancers yelled.

"Oh, my God! Apply pressure to it!"

When I noticed the bloody towels, I finally realized that I was the one who had been assaulted. I saw the horror on the dancers' faces and could only imagine how bad my injury was. I sent a prayer up to heaven. I did not want to die in the back of that limousine. I never thought my life would end from a random assault. I hadn't started a family yet and there was so much I wanted to accomplish. I continued to pray and ask God to keep me safe.

We must have gotten to the hospital in record time. I was still floating into and out of consciousness. I couldn't walk straight so the driver and the dancers helped me into the emergency room. The paramedics were waiting for us when we arrived. They immediately rushed me to the trauma center and started working on me.

My road manager had received word about the assault and hurried to the hospital to be with me. A few minutes later Gus arrived. The doctors wanted everyone to keep me alert. They feared that I could slip into a coma and possibly never wake again, Gus and Markey-Dew continued to talk to me while the doctors and nurses worked on my head.

They performed a number of x-rays and conducted a cat scan to discover the extent of my injuries. I sat on the edge of the hospital bed and waited for the results. AL waited in the room with me. My head throbbed. My hearing was muffled. Every time I spoke it felt like I was talking under water. I started to get nervous and wanted to see my injury. I removed the towel from my head and showed Gus.

"What does it look like?" I nervously asked.

The expression on his face told the whole story. AL was speechless. I walked to the mirror in the bathroom to take a look. I had to see it for myself before the doctors stitched me up. My mouth just fell open the minute I saw the injury. The ugly hole in my head was massive. I couldn't believe my eyes. I exploded into tears.

"Oh, my God!" I cried out.

I couldn't understand how something like this could happen to me. I started sobbing uncontrollably and asking why a man would do something like this to me. I was only four feet and eleven inches tall and every bit of one hundred and twenty pounds. For a man that large to deal me such a harsh gash was unreal. I became hysterical. The nurses urged me to settle down. They warned me that if I didn't calm myself that my body could seize up and I could slip into a coma and, possibly, die. I took heed to the warning and sat down on the hospital bed.

God was undoubtedly on my side that evening. The results came back from the x-rays and the CAT scan. One of the doctors calmly walked into the room to deliver the news.

"You are one lucky lady," The doctor said with a smile. "Don't worry. We are going to sew you up nice and pretty. There is no brain trauma or brain injury, just the split skin. There will be a scar but we are going to show you how to take care of it once we get you all stitched up. But I do have to tell you this young lady. You are very lucky," the doctor continued. "Thank God you had those braids in your hair because they absorbed most of the impact from the bottle. Even though the scalp spilt from the glass, those braids sustained most of the impact. If you didn't have those braids in your hair there's a strong possibility that the injury would have been a lot worse and you could've died."

The news immediately humbled me. Ironically, my

"Superwoman" braids came to my rescue that evening. A strong feeling of gratitude came over me. I felt lucky to be alive. A few minutes later, I was finally able to talk to my dad. He calmly prayed for me and told me everything was going to be okay.

"Why is this happening, Dad?" I cried to him. "My album is coming out in just a few days. I can't believe this happened to me."

"It's okay, kiddo. You're going to be okay," my dad reassured me. "The enemy doesn't want to see you win. Everything will be okay."

I really needed to hear my daddy's calming voice in that moment. The doctors were preparing to stitch me up and I felt anxious. My dad always knew what I needed to hear to keep my spirits high.

Two hours and twenty-three stitches later, I was released from the hospital. The doctors cleared me to fly and I was ready to escape San Francisco. I needed to get back home and be around my family. The doctors prescribed me strong medication and I was discharged. We all headed back to the hotel and got prepared to return to the east coast.

There's an old saying that bad news travels fast. In the music industry, bad news travels at light speed. The details about the assault started buzzing around the entertainment world. One of my first calls came from Jay Brown and Missy Elliott. They reached out to make sure that I was okay. I told them I was fine and that I would be traveling back to Baltimore the next morning. Missy assured me that she would be there for me if I needed anything.

After I hung up with Jay and Missy, my phone started ringing non-stop. It seemed like half the world was calling to check in on me. People were upset. Even people I didn't know personally were prepared to hunt down the guy who assaulted me. News outlets started posting the story online and releasing the details on the networks. I tried to calm everyone down and let them know I was okay. I really just wanted to get home to my family.

The next day I made it back safely to Baltimore. The flight was long and painful. I felt a lot of pressure on my head during the trip. When I got home I tried to relax but the pain was severe. The doctors told me I would experience some swelling but nothing could prepare me for the way my face ballooned as a result of the injury. I couldn't recognize myself in the mirror. My eyes were blackened and my head was swollen beyond belief. I looked like a damned monster. There was no way I could be seen in public even with my album due out in a few days. I thought my face would be stuck like this forever. It was an ugly sight. I cried every day. Then, I became angry. I started feeling like somebody set me up. A million questions swirled in my mind.

"Why did that dude only attack me? Why was I the only one hit? Why didn't he rob me? Why would somebody attack me at an R&B concert?"

The following weeks were rough. The violent episode had taken a mental toll on me and changed my perspective on life and my career. After all the hard work I put into this album, it hurt to know that I couldn't promote it. I had worked with so many different artists and had done so many favors in the past. I had no idea why something so heinous could happen to me. It felt unfair that I would be on the sidelines during the most important time of my career.

The news of the assault was still buzzing and my fans

responded by supporting my album. They made sure I had a successful release but it was hard for me to celebrate. I had to cancel all upcoming appearances. It was nearly impossible for me to promote my album.

The swelling on my head eventually subsided but then I had to face another tough reality. The image that I presented to my fans would never be seen again. The signature Lil' Mo braids, the colored corn rolls and the ombré hairstyles were dead. The large scar had cut deep into my hairline just above my eye. The hair would never grow back there. My attacker not only tried to kill me, but he tried to murder my Lil Mo' character.

I spent the next few months trying to come up with a plan to re-invent Lil' Mo. As an artist, I had to accept the fact that once I changed my hairstyle, it would be hard for the fans to recognize me. I still had all the tattoos but the label execs wanted me to cover them up because of main stream media. It was a tough comeback for Lil' Mo. From everyone seeing me with the signature braids in "Superwoman" to now wearing a bang and my hair out in the "Gangsta" video, it was definitely a huge change. Despite the challenges, Lil' Mo and my career survived, but Cynthia Loving would never be the same.

Before I was attacked, I was easily accessible to my fans and somewhat naïve to the dangers of living such a public life. I allowed people to approach me at will. Other celebrities tried to warn me about the risks I was taking with my life. I remember Wendy Williams pulling me to the side and warning me about making myself vulnerable to attacks.

"Don't hang around and meander when you're out in public." Wendy said to me. "Don't even go to the bathroom by yourself."

"Why do you say that?" I asked.

"Don't you know how fast somebody can slice your face, attack you, or even kill you in a bathroom?" Wendy said. "Stop doing that."

Her advice has stuck with me. After the assault, I changed the way I maneuvered in public. I got rid of my old bodyguards and hired the Nation of Islam to handle my security. I didn't make a move without them. I didn't trust a soul.

Before the assault, I would go out to all types of events and smile in everybody's face like they were my friend. All of that changed. I became guarded. I started watching people more closely and being mindful of my surroundings. I wouldn't go to the mall, out to dinner, or even to a public restroom without somebody I trusted. I became paranoid. Some days I thought I saw the guy who assaulted me. I scanned the crowds at my shows and swore he was somewhere out there, stalking me. I didn't know what to think. The San Francisco police department never caught the guy. It is still a mystery as to who was behind such a random act of violence.

Even today I'm deeply affected by the assault. When people approach me in public I become very alert and protective. People think I'm being shady when they notice me becoming cautious. They don't know that my defense mechanism immediately goes off when I'm approached by a stranger. I have to ask myself, *why is this person here? Is he or she here to attack me*? I have to be on guard at all times. If I ever feel threatened or like someone is maliciously trying to attack me, I go into beast mode. Regardless if it's in public, at an event, or even on the internet, my goal is to protect myself, my property and my family.

I learned a lot about people and the music industry after that fateful night. It hurt me to see how many people were laughing at my pain. A lot of people were spreading rumors that we were partying in a rowdy club and somebody tossed a bottle at me. Other people were joking that I deserved to be attacked because of my "gangsta" record and Lil' Mo persona. I couldn't believe how insensitive and cynical people could get. I had to learn the hard way that not everyone who smiles in my face is my friend.

I was once told that some of the people who yell your name the loudest only do so because they want to see you stumble. Some people will pose as your friend just to make you comfortable so they can walk around your wall and see you fall. I had to learn the hard way that a lot of people may know my name but they don't know me. They don't know my story and they don't know how hard I worked to get where I am. I learned that there are some people out there that don't have respect for my life and the things I want to accomplish. So I had to make it a priority to protect my life and my family.

A powerful message was burned into my mind after being assaulted. I started to treat my music career differently. I realized that no one was going to hold my hand through the entire ordeal. People called to check up on me and my family was there for me, but I had to dig deep to find the strength to get back on my feet and get back out there to pursue my dreams. I fought through the pounding headaches, the emotional struggles, and bouts with depression. Coming so close to death made me take a hard look at my priorities and refocus my energy. Knowing I could have died before I even started a family was a major wake up call for me. I love my career and I love what I do, but I learned during that rough time that I was not willing to die for this music industry because the music industry would surely never die for me.

*

PART III

Pain and Paper

Chapter Fifteen

The summer of 2001 was a very emotional time for me. I tried to be excited about the release of my debut album but it was difficult for me to keep my spirits up. Being assaulted on the West Coast had left me paranoid, angry, and abnormally depressed. The deep wound on my head was slowly healing but the questions surrounding the attack were still on my mind. I believed that God was trying to send me a message. The demands of my career forced me to live a fast lifestyle. I was moving a million miles per minute with no desire to slow down, but after the painful wakeup call I was forced to reevaluate my life.

Leaving this earth before I started a family was a harsh fate to imagine. I had accomplished a lot in the industry but I was still missing some things in my life. Ever since I was a child, I wanted to be a wife and a mother. Growing up and watching the love that my parents shared made me want to live a similar life. I wanted to be happily married with a big, loving family. All of those childhood fantasies were almost wiped away in a blink of an eye. The assault gave me a new outlook on life and God's message to me was heard loud and clear: slow down.

Before the assault, my then boyfriend and I barely discussed the topic of marriage. Augustus "AL" Stone was my best friend, my manager, and my lover. Earlier that year, I met AL during a very busy time in my life. I was working on my first album and doing numerous shows to stay in the spotlight. A boyfriend was the last thing I was looking for at the time. I had a lot going on in my professional career and having a man was at the bottom of the list. I wasn't looking for love but it seemed that love was looking for me. AL and I were from different worlds. That was evident from the very first day we met.

Our story began in the parking lot of a gas station. One afternoon my sister, Charese, and I were running errands in Maryland. We pulled into a gas station to fill up and AL was parked in front of us. My sister nudged me and smiled.

"That's the guy I was telling you about," Charese said. "I know you seen him before. That's the dude that was trying to holla at you."

"Who is that?" I snapped. "I don't know him."

I tried to brush my sister off but she was persistent. I didn't have time for any guys. I was trying to focus on my career.

"Nah, he's mad cool," Charese said. "He got a lot of cars and houses and he knows how to flip them."

"What?" I shook my head. "That sounds like some 'hood nigga shit to me."

Charese and I shared a quick laugh. My sister told me more about AL and pled for me to meet him. As we continued to talk, AL walked over to my truck. I was impressed by his confidence. AL was not afraid to talk to me. I could tell immediately that he was a street dude.

"So, what y'all doing tonight?" AL asked.

"I got a show tonight in DC with Ja Rule," I responded. "You tryin' to come?"

"Yes," he quickly said.

I'm not sure why I invited AL out that night but something told me to give him a shot. I wasn't used to men approaching me in public but his confidence was something that I respected. I told AL that I didn't know my way around DC and was clueless where the club was located. AL agreed to pick me up later that evening. He said he wanted to make sure that we made it to the club safely. I gave AL my address. I told him to be at my house by 9:00pm so I wouldn't be late for the show.

Later that evening I was getting dressed in my bedroom. It was 9:30pm and AL hadn't arrived at my house yet. I didn't know much about AL at the time and he was already making a bad first impression. I had just finished showering and was getting dressed when my bedroom door flew open. I spun around in a panic and noticed it was AL standing at my door.

"Yoooo!" I yelled. "What the hell is wrong with you? Who just busts in someone's room, yo?"

I was standing in the middle of the room completely nude.

"Oh, I'm sorry," AL stuttered and fumbled to close the door.

I yelled for Charese and she rushed upstairs to my room.

"What the hell?" I yelled at her. "What is he doing?

He can't be coming in my room like that."

"Nah, that's my bad," Charese said. "I thought you was dressed. He wanted to apologize for being late."

"I understand that but he can't be coming in my room like that," I said. "I could've been doing anything in here. See? He think he too cool already. I can see that this ain't gonna work."

I was clearly upset with AL and he apologized to me. Charese made him wait downstairs until I finished getting dressed. I tried to calm myself down but I was irked. AL was already working with two strikes, one for being late and one for barging into my room. He was holding on by a thread.

I calmed myself down and walked downstairs. A few minutes later, we all left for DC and headed to the club. AL was driving his SUV and he wanted to make amends for being late.

"Y'all want something to drink?" AL asked.

Before I could respond to the question, he pulled out a bottle of Remy. He placed the dark liquor in his cup holder and continued driving. As he slammed on his brakes, the drink spilled directly onto my lap and all over my outfit.

"Oh, my God!" I screamed.

AL had officially pissed me off for the evening. That was his third strike. I hadn't known him for a full twenty four hours and he was already on my "I can't do this" list. Not only was I late for my show but now AL spilled liquor all on my clothes. I was beyond over him. I was ready to get this awkward night over with. A few hours later, AL dropped us off back at my house. My performance was a success and I was exhausted.

"So, am I gonna see you again?" AL asked. "Probably

not," I said. "I got a lot going on right now."

"Well, we can keep in touch, right?" AL said to me.

"I don't know," I responded. "This is my business phone and I really don't like talking on the phone like that." He didn't take no for an answer that evening.

"I tell you what. I will get you a phone," AL suggested. "That way you can have your own phone. We can get a family plan."

"Family plan?" I asked him.

"Yea, I can get the phones and I will pay for them," AL said.

"Okay, but I have to leave for New York tomorrow early morning," I explained. "If you get the phones by tomorrow then we can talk."

I could tell that AL was serious about getting to know me. The next day he showed up to my house with three phones. He gave one to me. He even bought a phone for Charese and my good friend, Carlos. I was impressed by AL's thoughtfulness. We spoke for a few minutes and then I left for New York.

Later that evening, I was relaxing at the Time Hotel in New York City. I received a call on my new phone and realized it was AL. I figured he was calling to check in on me but I would soon find out that AL was full of surprises.

"Which hotel are you guys staying at?" he asked.

"I'm at the Time Hotel." I replied. "Why?"

"I will be there in a few minutes." AL said.

I couldn't believe my ears. AL drove all the way to New York and popped in on me. The phone call made me slightly nervous and I didn't know how to react.

"What are you doing here, stalker?" I asked AL when he arrived at the hotel.

"I know you said you needed to get on the road and I wanted to make sure you was okay," AL said.

His response made me smile but it also made me leery. AL knew I was an entertainer and I wasn't sure how to respond to his aggressiveness. My sister and I started jokingly referring to AL as "the stalker," but she insisted that he was cool.

AL and I started hanging out regularly after that day. We became good friends and I would see AL whenever I came off the road. The more we learned about each other the closer we became. AL was a quiet guy but he was clearly from the streets. I liked that he had rough edges but smooth ways. I had met a lot of people in the industry who pretended to be tough guys, but AL seemed to be the real deal. I felt comfortable when I was around him. It took roughly three months for me to warm up to him but, before long, AL and I were a couple. We did everything together. We enjoyed each other's company so much that I started taking AL on the road with me. He was my friend first and we had a lot of fun times.

After just a few short months our relationship began to grow. AL started to help me out a lot more with my career. He used to say that the music game was no different than the drug/street game. The goal was simply to make money. AL became my manager and he handled a lot of my affairs. Even when I went out on tour, AL would handle a lot of the business and make sure I didn't have to worry about much outside of performing. We traveled to a lot of cities together. These great times only made our relationship stronger.

Getting assaulted in San Francisco changed our relationship. It seemed that AL and I had experienced some extreme highs and very extreme lows together. I knew it was tough for AL to see me nearly lose my life. The emotional strain on the both of us began to show, but, instead of pulling away from each other, AL and I became closer and stronger. Our love for each other was deep and there was only one thing left to do.

"So are you trying to be my wife or what?"

It wasn't the most romantic proposal that I envisioned when I was a child but AL was not a traditional type of person. In August of 2001, AL surprised me with his request for my hand in marriage. We were taking a break from the road but we were slated to head back out in a few days. The proposal was impromptu and I was stunned by his question. My heart fluttered before I answered. This was something that I had wanted my entire life. I had been thinking about this day for a while so my decision was an easy one. I accepted. Nothing could wipe the smile off of my face. I was emotional. I knew this was a big step for the both of us but I did not want to wait. I suggested to AL that we take advantage of our break and get married as soon as possible.

"This week?" AL asked.

"Yes, why not?" I responded. "We can get married before I head back out on tour."

Although it was very short notice, he agreed to the idea. We planned to get married in less than forty eight hours in the lower level of my townhouse. We had no time to plan a huge ceremony so we decided to invite thirty of our closest relatives and friends to our secret wedding.

AL and I woke up early that next morning. There was a lot to get done. We started the day by heading down to City Hall in Annapolis, Maryland, to secure our marriage license. We then sent out text messages, made phones calls, and invited our friends and family over to the house for what we called a special ceremony. People responded immediately with joy and excitement. There was going to be a great turnout. We wanted to this to be a day we would never forget.

AL and I lived in a townhome with a finished basement. We scrambled to get wedding decorations to make our home look nice for our guests. We bought white roses to throw down the steps and borrowed three dozen fold-up chairs from my father's church. We didn't have time to cook for a reception so we called in a favor from AL's cousin, Lance London. Lance owned a huge restaurant chain in the area called Carolina Kitchen. His recipes were amazing and we knew he would be the perfect person to make sure our guests enjoyed the dinner.

Soon, it was time for me to find a dress. I owned a few dresses and nice pant suits but for my wedding day I wanted to wear something that I had never worn before. I headed to the mall to find a dress before the stores closed. It was August and the bridal season was winding down. I was searching for something that was nice and on sale. I didn't mind spending the money but I didn't see the use of splurging because we were doing a private wedding in the basement of my home.

After spending hours in stores like Macy's and David's Bridal I came up empty. I searched a few smaller stores and I didn't find anything I liked. A few minutes later I was ready to give up. I told my sister Charese that I would just wear something from my closet. We headed to the exit of the mall and walked through JC Penny. Before we could leave the building a dress caught my eye.

"Yooo, that's the dress!" I screamed.

I looked it over and became excited. The dress was a size four and it was perfect for me. The dress was not pure white. It was a shade between mother-of-pearl and egg-shell white. I loved it. I glanced down at the tag and it was nearly eighty percent off. After all the mark downs and discounts the final price was fifteen dollars. I had a twenty-dollar bill on me so I knew that this was destined to be.

Charese and I rushed back home with the wedding decorations and my fifteen-dollar-dress in tow. My brothers and my sister helped us decorate the basement and get everything prepared. I fired up my computer and worked on the wedding program. I was far from a graphic designer but I whipped something together and printed the programs out on our home printer. We even ran out of ink so we rushed over to the twenty-four hour Wal-Mart to get more ink to get the rest of them done.

The next morning we all were exhausted. Preparing for the last minute wedding had taken a lot out of us, but we were far from done. My family came over and helped us get the rest of the house in order. Charese and I grabbed some last minute things and I prepared myself to take the big plunge. Then, my phone rang.

"So, you ready to do this?" AL asked me.

"I am," I replied. "Are you ready?"

"Yes," AL responded.

We were young lovers at the time but we were prepared to take the life-long journey of being husband and wife. Charese and I finished up the preparations and we were ready for the ceremony. Because it's bad luck for the groom to see the bride before the wedding, AL had left the house while I got dressed. He owned a townhouse five minutes away in the same community. The next time he was to see me was in my basement later that evening.

A few hours later, our family and friends started arriving at the house. Despite the short notice, everyone arrived with gifts. My family even brought a cake for us. Everyone was filing into the basement while I was in my bedroom getting dressed. My sister helped me get ready and finished off my hair. I did my own makeup and even put rhinestones on my face. I'm sure it looked like a mess but I thought it was cute. I took one final look at myself in the mirror. I still couldn't believe I was about to get married. The butterflies in my stomach were going crazy but it was no time to be nervous. It was finally time to tie the knot.

My sister told me that everyone was ready. I didn't have a bridal party so my sister volunteered to walk me downstairs. My father agreed to do the service. I walked to the top of the stairs and I could hear my father saying the prayer to open up the ceremony. A few minutes later the basement was completely silent. Everyone stood up and waited for me to make my grand appearance. I hesitated when I noticed the music wasn't playing.

"Can somebody press play?" Charese yelled downstairs.

Someone rushed over to the stereo and played the music. "Differences" by Ginuwine played through the speakers. I slowly walked down the stairs and was greeted by a proud and excited group of friends and family. The basement looked beautiful with all the flowers and balloons.

My father and AL stood in front of our improvised altar near the fireplace. My groom-to-be was sharply dressed in a tuxedo. I slowly walked towards him and smiled at all the guests.

"Wow, you look beautiful," he said as I stood in front of him.

"You look alright," I joked and smiled at him.
My father waited for the song to go off and then he began the ceremony.

"Is there anyone among us that objects to this union?" My dad asked.

We both turned around and glared at our friends with a playful dirty look. Everyone started laughing. There were no objectors. I nudged my father and told him that my younger brother James was going to sing for us before we said our vows. My father invited James to the floor to perform.

When I looked at my brother, I could tell that something was not right. The previous evening I asked James to sing "Love" by Musiq Soulchild. He was honored to be a part of the ceremony. What we didn't know was that James had smoked a bag of weed just before the ceremony. He tried to keep his composure but he was buzzed and everybody knew it

"*Looooovvvvve... so many things I got to tell ya* – my throat is so dry."

James coughed and struggled through the song. My brother tried to sing the song but he was struggling.

"*...but I'm afraid I don't know how* – oh my God I'm so high," my brother said laughing.

James apologized through the entire song. Everyone in the basement was laughing as my brother turned his singing performance into a comedy routine. When his big note came James was too high to continue. Everyone gave him a sarcastic round of applause and told him to have a seat.

After my brother sat down it was time for the exchanging of vows. My father completed the ceremony and we kissed for the first time as husband and wife. Our family and friends applauded the new union. Instead of playing a traditional wedding song, we played a Jay-Z track and headed for the exit. Before we left we threw up our deuces to everyone and walked out of the basement.

Our ceremony was nothing short of a "ghetto wedding" but we loved every minute of it. Everyone in attendance had a ball and my parents were very proud of us. AL and I were best friends and it didn't matter to us where we exchanged our vows. We were surrounded by great friends, a beautiful family, and unconditional love.

*

Chapter Sixteen

"What do you want for Christmas?" my husband asked me.

"I want to be pregnant for Christmas," I responded.

AL and I had been married for nearly three months and just like all newlyweds the euphoria of our union kept us on a natural high. Since the wedding, we travelled on the road a lot and promoted my debut album. News of our wedding spread and everyone congratulated us. It felt good to be married to AL. I felt safer. I believed that AL would be more diligent in his responsibility to protect me. A lot had been happening in 2001 that made me a nervous wreck. The beautiful songstress Aaliyah passed away, the Twin Towers were attacked by terrorists, and earlier that year I was assaulted in San Francisco. With all that was going on in the world, I didn't want to wait to start our family.

While having a conversation about the upcoming holidays, AL asked me what I wanted for Christmas. I didn't want any material things from my new husband. Our home was already cluttered with gadgets and things for people who have everything. I wanted a gift from my husband that I had desired my entire life. I wanted a child.

"Are you sure?" AL asked me.

"Yes, I'm sure," I responded. "We have been doing enough practicing. It's time for us to start a family. I will wait to take the test on Christmas Day. If I'm pregnant, then that will be your gift to me."

AL agreed.

On Christmas morning in 2001, I woke up early and took a pregnancy test. AL and I were elated when the test came back positive. I screamed for joy. AL was already a father of two other children, one from a one-night stand and one from a previous marriage, but he was proud and excited that we were celebrating the coming of our own child. I told my family immediately and couldn't wait to show them my pregnancy test. Not only were we a married couple but AL and I were only months away from becoming parents together.

We shared the news with our families but we told them to keep it a secret. Cynthia Loving had to have this child, but Lil' Mo had to continue to be the artist. I was nervous to tell the record label so I decided to break the news after the New Year. I was in my first trimester and I didn't want to cause any problems with the pregnancy.

I first broke the news to my product manager at the label. I was expecting a negative response. I even prepared myself to be dropped by the label, but the execs were surprisingly excited for me. In the past, music execs encouraged their artists to hide their pregnancies, but my label embraced my news. AL told them that we were going to take a break from the road in order to put less stress on my body. The plan was to record the new album while I prepared myself for the birth of my first child.

A few months into my pregnancy I heard from my friend Phil Thornton that a radio station in the Baltimore area was searching for new talent. I didn't have much experience on the radio, besides filling in at times on HOT 97. I had no formal training, but with my name buzzing in the industry I knew I would have a good shot at bringing a new voice to the airwaves. The Program Director at the time was Thea Mitchum. She loved "The Lil' Mo Show" concept and even without an air check she immediately hired me. Thea Mitchum helped to make my radio experience a successful one. I will be forever grateful for her faith in me.

Things seemed to be clearing an easy path for the birth of my first child. I was spared the rigorous grind of heading out on tour and performing on the road. For the next seven months of my pregnancy, I hosted a midday radio set called "The Lil Mo Show." From the first day I hit the air, the show was a winner. We boosted the moral of the community and the show became number one in our time slot.

As my pregnancy moved along I also stayed active in the music world. I shot a music video for a song I recorded with Angie Martinez called "If I Can Go." I made sure to be a part of the Angie Martinez video because I knew it would be the final video before I had my child. During my pregnancy, I also started working on songs for my second album called "Meet the Girl Next Door." I recorded the song "Ten Commandments" with Lil' Kim and also recorded the hit single "4ever." Although I was married when I wrote and recorded "4ever," I was still ecstatic and overjoyed at the fact that I was a wife and soon to be a mother. The lyrics were very personal and I believe that's why the fans instantly took to the song. I spent four months recording my second album. The emotions I was experiencing were very real and people still relate to the passion in the music.

In August of 2002, I was just weeks away from having my first child. Outside of doing the radio show and recording the album I did everything in my power to have a healthy pregnancy. I took Lamaze classes and tried to keep my stress to a minimum. Earlier that summer, I experienced a scare. One evening, I started bleeding and I felt like I was having complications. I immediately thought back to my miscarriage in 1996 and began to panic. My heart was pounding like a bass drum. I was scared to go to the hospital fearing that I would experience the same nightmare as I had when I was just a teen. I was a lot further along this time around and I had even felt my baby kick. I started to feel like there was a spirit that was trying to take my baby away.

I called the nurse helpline to see if I could get an explanation for the bleeding. I was told to try and relax and, if possible, to elevate my feet.

"Do you see clotting? Or, do you have a fever?" The nurse asked me.

"No, I'm just spotting." I nervously responded.

The nurse proceeded to tell me that I was experiencing nothing out of the ordinary. She advised me to relax and to head to the hospital if the bleeding persisted. I called my parents when I hung up with the helpline. My mom and dad lived seven minutes away. They rushed over to check in on me. My parents calmed my spirit and we had prayer. I asked God to watch over my unborn child. I decided to get some rest and try to relax my body. I was nearly in tears thinking about the possibility of losing another child. I slept for a few hours and began to calm down. I was relieved when I woke up and noticed that the bleeding had stopped.

Despite the scare I still remained very active during the final weeks of my pregnancy. I didn't want to lie around all day. I believed that if I had a lethargic pregnancy then I would have a lethargic child and I didn't want that. Even as I came down to the final days of my pregnancy, I tried to remain as busy as possible.

My due date was August 21, 2002, but I started having contractions two days early. My stomach was cramping and I felt like I was in labor, but I wasn't sure. A few hours before my water broke I was doing everything from playing double-dutch to hanging at my sister's job at Circuit City. Later that day, I decided to do my mother's hair just to keep myself busy. There was something about the sound of a loud blow dryer that kept my mind off of the pain. The contractions were now coming more frequently.

In the middle of doing my mother's hair, a harsh pain ripped through my stomach. The severe contraction almost made me drop the blow dryer. I grabbed my belly and contemplated going to the hospital. I decided to take a shower to see if the pain would ease, but the pain had gotten worse. While I was in the bathroom, my mucus plug was dispelled and I knew it was time for me to rush to the hospital. My baby was coming.

I was thrilled, anxious and scared. I quickly got dressed and grabbed my bag. My mother called my family and called all of the saints from the church. We rushed to the hospital in record time. I wanted everything to go smoothly for my first child. Everyone was excited for me. It was still unbelievable that Little Cindy was about to become a mother. The nurse immediately checked my status and told me that I was at five centimeters. They admitted me and made the preparations for my delivery.

The pain intensified by the minute. I felt like someone was chopping the side of my body with a dull ax. I couldn't believe it. There wasn't a blow dryer big enough that could help me ignore the pain. Everyone in the room tried to calm me down, but I didn't want to hear anybody talk. The pain consumed me to the point that I wanted to punch a wall or try to bite through a piece of steel. I just wanted the pain to be over. The doctors decided to give me an epidural to make me more comfortable.

After another status report I found out that my cervix was only at seven centimeters. I was becoming exhausted. Everyone tried to keep my spirits high but I could tell that they were growing impatient. A few hours later, I was fully dilated. While the doctor was checking my cervix she uttered something unexpected.

"Where's the baby's head?" The doctor asked.

"What?" I quickly yelled. "What do you mean where's my baby's head?"

The doctor told me that my baby crawled deeper into my body. I would need an emergency Cesarean. I nearly panicked in the hospital room. It seemed that my baby was going to be just as stubborn as I was when I was born. The medical staff wheeled me into another room to perform the surgery. My heart was racing out of control. The anesthesiologist on duty tried to calm me down.

"Don't worry," he said. "This is probably going to be the easiest procedure you ever had. I am going to give you something to slow your heart rate down because you are very anxious right now."

"Yea, okay," I nervously said, "but they said they can't find my baby's head. Where's my baby's head?"

No matter how much the staff tried to relieve my fears, I was exceedingly nervous. The medicine began to kick in and my body started going numb. The doctors performed the cesarean while I was in and out of the twilight. In the middle of the procedure, I felt them pulling and tugging on my body. I remember hearing one doctor call for suction. I later learned that my baby was so far under my rib cage that she had to be vacuumed out, but no matter how hard she tried to fight it, my daughter, Heaven Love'on Stone, was finally born on August 19, 2002.

My daughter's first cries were the sweetest sounds I ever had heard. The reality of being a mother hit me. The moment I had been waiting on my entire life had finally arrived. I couldn't have been any happier. The nurses cleaned my daughter and handed her to me. I was overcome with emotion. All I could do was smile. Despite my elation, my daughter's expression was the total opposite. She gave me a scowl that I will never forget. I know my daughter couldn't speak at the time but she looked at me and frowned as if to say, "*Mom, you could've left me inside there. I was chillin'.*"

Thinking about my daughter's first expression still makes me laugh. Since the moment she was born, I just wanted to give her the world. Having a family has always been my lifelong dream. AL and I shared a deep moment of connection after my daughter was born. I couldn't thank him enough for giving me something that I longed for my entire life. From that day forward it would be my family and me against the world.

*

Chapter Seventeen

Image is everything in the music industry. You would be hard pressed to find any performer who is not concerned about his or her style and appearance. The competition for the spotlight is fierce. People will do, and have done, just about anything to gain fame in the music world. I never looked at myself as a person that would alter her body or change her face for the sake of gaining more fans. I always considered myself to be a real person. I learned at an early age that I was born with a God-given talent. I always wanted to stay true to my gifts and use my talents to break into the music business. For the longest time I never let the pressure to succeed hinder me from having a successful career. In 2004, the strong belief and confidence I had in myself was tested. The seductive nature of the industry got the best of me and caused me to question my own identity as an artist. A seemingly innocent conversation about ten pounds would nearly cost me my life.

After giving birth to my first daughter in 2002, it seemed like I was accomplishing everything I wanted in life. I had a great career. I was married and I finally had started a family of my own. Nothing could come close to the euphoria of motherhood. I had recorded my second album entitled "Meet the Girl Next Door" and was excited to share my joy with the world.

But as I prepared myself to drop another solo project I noticed that I was having a hard time losing the baby weight I gained. I was eating right and exercising but nothing seemed to be working. I was hovering around 130 pounds at the time. Because of my short stature, the extra weight made me look thick. I wanted to be down to my pre-baby weight of 117 pounds. After a year of trying diets, body shapers and even personal trainers, I noticed that I was losing the weight slowly. Still, I was nowhere near my ideal weight. I started growing agitated and worried. I felt the added pounds were going to affect my career. I had seen the music industry swallow a lot of girls up and I didn't want to fall victim to the heartless nature of the business. The last thing I wanted to do was be replaced by a thinner version of myself.

In 2002, I was signed to Violator Management. They were the best management company in the industry. They kept me busy with performances and shows. They made sure I was visible and constantly in the public's eye. I also worked with a number of stylists who kept me in the trendiest clothes. They would give me the smallest sizes or what's commonly referred to as the sample sizes. Those extra small sizes always looked good for photo shoots, videos and events, but with my new baby-weight I started running into issues with those sample sizes. I always had hips and I always had a ghetto booty, but now I had a few extra pounds to contend with. After a while the word got back to me that I needed to lose weight. During a meeting with the executives at Violator

Management, the late Chris Lighty spoke to me briefly about my image.

"Mo, I overheard a few people suggesting that maybe you should lose about ten pounds before your album comes out," Chris said to me. "It will make your image more identifiable."

I thought to myself, *they have no idea how hard I am working to drop the weight.* I was far from being fat but I was trying my best to get back to my slim look. I left the meeting very annoyed. I had my daughter, Heaven, with me and I was fuming as we waited in the lobby for my car. I allowed the meeting to get under my skin and a few weeks later I found myself succumbing to the pressures of the industry. I knew a lot of music artists were getting plastic surgeries and secret work done to their bodies. I didn't want to get anything major but I didn't want to take a chance of being replaced. I decided it was time to make a major move. It was time for me to go under the knife.

In the early part of 2004, I elected to have two procedures done. I decided to get liposuction and a rhinoplasty for my nose. I paid $7,500 for my liposuction surgery and put down a deposit of $800 for my nose job. I was looking at a total of over $11,000 for my surgeries. I truly believed that my career was in jeopardy so money was not an issue. I immediately scheduled the liposuction first and my plan was to get my nose done following my recovery.

A few weeks later the big day arrived. I was instructed to fast the night before in preparation for my early morning surgery so I made sure not to eat a thing. I asked my father to drop me off at the cosmetic surgery facility in Maryland. As always, my dad was in my corner. It was going to be a quick in-and-out surgery and I felt more comfortable having my father with me. My dad has always been a careful driver and I knew he would get me there safely. When we arrived at the facility I decided to go in alone and asked my father to return in a few hours to pick me up.

As the nurses prepped me for surgery they went over the pros and cons of the procedure. I was informed that there was a chance that the fat could come back in different places once it was removed from my stomach area. A few nurses didn't understand why I was getting liposuction at such an early age. I didn't mind the questions because they had no idea what kind of pressure I was under as a recording artist. The staff also warned me about the side effects of the anesthesia. They told me I could become nauseated and sick from the medication. Despite the risks, I signed off on everything and the doctors proceeded with the surgery.

After the procedure, I woke up in tears. I had no clue what was going on. I couldn't feel a thing but the anesthesia had my mind in a state.

"Where am I?" I cried out. "What am I doing in the hospital?"

The nurses immediately calmed me down and brought me back to reality.

"You just had liposuction surgery and everything went well," one of the nurses said. "Once we stabilize all of your levels you will be discharged and free to go."

I was relieved to hear that the surgery was successful. The nurses placed a huge bandage around my stomach and waist. They discussed the recovery process and one of the doctors prescribed some pain medication. About an hour later I was discharged. My parents decided to stay at my house to help me recover.

I started feeling a lot of pain in my stomach a few hours after my surgery. My parents reminded me that I had gotten major abdominal surgery on top of just having a baby a little over a year ago. They said I was putting a lot of physical stress on my body. I tried to take comfort in their words but my stomach was killing me. I tried to use the bathroom but every time I tried to go nothing would happen. I took the first round of medicine but the pain only seemed to get worse with each passing hour.

The next day the pain was even more severe and I still couldn't use the bathroom. It felt like my bowels were not working and I couldn't figure out what was going on. My temperature was slowly climbing. My father took one look at me and he could tell that something was wrong.

"You don't look so good, kiddo," my dad said. "Are you feeling okay?"

"Not really." I responded. "I don't feel well."

"Maybe you need to put something on your stomach," my dad suggested. "It may just be the medicine."

I tried to eat something but I couldn't keep anything down. My parents took my temperature. I had a temperature of close to 102 degrees. My stomach looked bigger than it was the day before. I figured it was because I was sitting around the house so I decided to get out and get some air. The first thing I decided to do was head out to get my feet done. I had been going to the same salon for years so I felt it would be a good place to relax and take my mind off the pain. As soon as I walked inside the shop I was confronted with a dose of reality.

"Ooooo, you are pregnant again! Are you having

another baby?" The nail tech smiled at me.

"Well, damn," I responded to her joke, "I actually just had liposuction and I guess this is the side effects."

I was embarrassed by the lady's reaction to my stomach. I had given birth to my daughter a little over a year ago and was shocked that the nail tech thought I was pregnant again. I looked down at my stomach. Something was clearly wrong with me.

I headed back home and my parents came back over to help out. I tried to eat a meal and I still couldn't keep anything down. I tried to drink some water but it was hard for me to swallow. I lay down on a heating pad and my stomach started hurting even worse. A few minutes later I felt a sharp pain from my midsection and I jumped up. I rushed to the bathroom and started vomiting. I spit up a thick black substance and felt my body go numb. The sight scared me. I knew it was time to head to the emergency room. I prayed that it was nothing serious.

My father drove me to Anne Arundel Medical Center. I always felt comfortable going to AAMC. I loved their professionalism and their ethics. I delivered my daughter Heaven there, so anytime I felt sick I trusted their staff. Because of my high fever, I was admitted immediately. The first test they conducted was a pregnancy test. I informed them that I was recovering from liposuction surgery and there was no way I could be pregnant. I told them that I was having difficulty using the bathroom and that my stomach was killing me.

After a few more tests one of the nurses approached me with the results. She told me that my bowels were not functioning at all. The serious news caused me to panic. I started asking a lot of questions. The nurses informed me that my bowels were dormant. They said I would have to stay in the hospital until my bowels started working again. They compared my situation to a clogged drain. The poison that my body was producing was getting backed up in my stomach. There was a possibility that my blood could get infected and I would be facing grave consequences. The news almost sent me into shock. The liposuction surgery had backfired. The surgery that was meant to save my career was now threatening to take my life.

The first two nights in the hospital were a nightmare. The nurses gave me medicine to drop my fever but nothing worked to get my bowels moving again. I could urinate without a problem, but it was impossible for me to defecate. Every day seemed to bring more and more pain. My body felt like it was deteriorating fast and so was my spirit. The young nurse that assisted me every morning tried to keep me in a positive mood but it was hard for me to stay optimistic. I didn't want my family to see me like this. I was ashamed and embarrassed about my condition. I started to feel like I deserved this punishment for trying to alter my body. By the third day in the hospital I was slowly giving up my will to live.

The plastic surgeon that performed my procedure came to see me on the third day. My bowels were still sleep and it seemed like even the professionals were running out of answers. He apologized for my condition and tried to console me.

"I am so sorry about all of this," The surgeon felt remorseful. "It's nobody's fault that this happened. These are some of the possible side effects. Statistically this happens very rarely."

"Exactly. This is just my luck. I should've just tried to lose weight the natural way." I was angry and clearly afraid. "This is exactly what I get for getting liposuction."

"No, this is not your fault," the surgeon said. "These are just some of the things that could happen. It could have been a blockage from your prior pregnancy or even the scar tissue. There could be a number of reasons for this."

As much as the surgeon tried to explain away the issue I still had to face a very grim reality. After three miserable days in the hospital, my bowels remained nonfunctioning. I still couldn't use the bathroom. The nurses and doctors grew more concerned about me. They feared that all of the solid waste and excrement in my stomach could begin to seep out and possibly come through my esophagus. Knowing I would be vulnerable to a number of infections and diseases they couldn't take a chance of that happening. They decided it was time to manually flush out my stomach.

The nurses tried to caution me about the pain of the procedure but nothing could prepare me for what was coming next. I watched them closely as they stretched out a long plastic tube about the size of my arm. They needed to run the tube through my nose and attach it to my stomach. They asked me to drink water as they slowly forced the tube into my nose and down my throat. The first attempt failed. My body rejected the tube. The pain was too intense. They removed the tube and repeated the procedure. I gathered my strength and drank the water as they pushed the tube through my nose once again. Tears fell from my eyes. I couldn't believe the pain. I felt the plastic tube slowly moving down my throat and attaching to my stomach. It felt like someone was stabbing me repeatedly with a sharp blade. The nurses taped the tube to the side of my face. I watched in disgust as all the waste and poison began to flow into a plastic bag next to me. Black feces, mucus, fluid and even chewing gum flowed into the bag. I grew sicker just watching it. I felt like I was in the middle of hell and there was no end in sight.

Things seemed to be getting worse for me every minute I was lying in the hospital bed. My health was dwindling fast and I felt miserable. My bowels were still nonfunctioning so the doctors decided it was time to do surgery. They were baffled by my symptoms and advised me that I would need to have part of my colon surgically removed to clear the blockage. They warned me that the operation was serious and I would be down for nearly six weeks. There was no guarantee that the surgery would work but it would help them diagnose the problem and prepare me if another surgery was necessary.

At this point, I was emotionally, physically, and spiritually exhausted. I had been on a liquid diet and crunching ice for most of my hospital stay. I could barely comprehend the severity of the news and I was losing my desire to see another day. The doctors scheduled the emergency surgery for that next morning. I wasn't sure that I would survive it.

I wanted to see my daughter, Heaven, so I asked my family to bring her up to the hospital. With all that was going on with me, I knew that seeing and holding my daughter would lift my spirits. She was a little over a year-old at the time and I knew her vibrant soul would put a smile on my face. My family brought her into my hospital room but she didn't recognize me.

"No….no…no…!" Heaven screamed.

Heaven refused to come to me. She didn't recognize me at all. She started crying as if I was a stranger. My baby's fearful reaction crushed me. My family tried to tell Heaven that I was her mother but she cried uncontrollably and shook her head. Seeing my daughter scream and sob made me cry. I tried to speak to her so that she could hear my voice. I wanted her to know that it was her mother calling for her and not some monster. I had lost a lot of weight and my skin was losing its normal complexion. No matter how hard I tried, Heaven refused to come to me. I was devastated.

My family stayed with me well after visiting hours were over. My family was there when the doctors gave me additional details of the surgery. The staff wanted to give me one more night of rest and see if my system would start working before they proceeded with the operation. They scheduled the surgery for first thing in the morning and they wanted me to rest up. Before my family left they all kissed and hug me. I started getting choked up as my mother hugged me.

"Well, if you don't see me tomorrow, mom, just know that I love you in real life," I cried as she left.

My father could tell I was out of it and he stayed with me for a few more minutes. He suggested that I walk around the hospital so I could get some fresh air. I didn't know if I had the strength but my dad convinced me to try. As we walked the halls, my father tried to encourage me with each step.

"Well, Dad, I guess this is what I get," I said as we slowly walked down the hall. "I'm sorry for all of this. I shouldn't have spent all of this money on something I knew wasn't going to work."

"It's okay. This is not your fault. You will be fine." My dad calmly said. "You have to *will* yourself back to health."

"What does that mean?" I snapped at my dad. "Right now, I don't even want to be alive. After the surgery I'm probably going to look crazy. My stomach is bruised up and black. My skin looks freakin' pale and gray. My face looks sunken in and I have a tube up my nose, but you are telling me to *will* myself back to health. Yeah right. Who can *will* themselves back to health?"

"You just have to believe, kiddo," my dad responded. He continued to work on my spirit and give me encouragement. As he spoke, we walked around the hospital floor a few more times.

"See, kiddo. You don't even realize what you are doing now." My father said. "You are walking a lot better now."

My dad's words made me feel better. As we headed back into my room we had prayer.

"Please, God, if you exist like I know you do, please let the doctors hear something when they come into this room tomorrow." I prayed like it was my last night on earth. "I promise not to do anything like this again. I can't keep living like this."

I asked my dad to come back in the morning. My surgery was going to be early and I wanted him to be there in case I had to stay in the hospital any longer. We embraced and he told me that he would see me in the morning.

I stayed up all night in the hospital room. I tried to watch the news and keep my mind off of the surgery. I hated being in the hospital alone. I tried to stay positive in order to make it through the night. I was ready to get back to work and get back to my family.

The next morning seemed to take an eternity to arrive. The young nurse who had been waiting on me during my entire stay walked into my room.

"How are you feeling, Cynthia?" The young nurse smiled at me. "Do you feel like you can use the bathroom?"

"I feel like I can, but I don't know. You tell me," I said.

I was exhausted from another night with no sleep. I had stayed up for most of the evening thinking about my operation. The nurse told me that she would check my system. She placed her stethoscope on my stomach and listened for any changes.

"Uh-oh," the young nurse sang.

"What?" I instantly grew nervous.

"I think I hear some movement," the nurse said with a smile.

"Are you serious?" I asked.

"I don't want to get too excited," the nurse said, "but let me get the doctor so he can confirm there is movement."
A few minutes later, the doctor came into my room with my chart.

"The nurse said she heard movement, but we don't want to get ahead of ourselves," the doctor explained. "It could be the sound of you clearing your throat or any type of internal sound. We just want to make sure."

After a few minutes of checking my system the doctor said, "Your bowels are moving. Do you feel like you can use the bathroom?"

"Yes." I quickly responded.

"Okay. We are going to remove the tube. If you can use the bathroom, then you can go home."

The nurses couldn't remove the tube fast enough. I rushed into the bathroom and took the largest shit I had ever taken in my life. The relief I felt was something I couldn't explain in words. I just sat there and cried. I knew I was the recipient of a miracle. An hour before I was scheduled to undergo surgery, my bowels started working again. The seven day ordeal was finally over.

I called my dad and he picked me up. I felt blessed to be discharged. I left the hospital with a different outlook on life. I canceled my nose job and let the doctor keep my deposit. It took me a while to forgive myself for buckling to the pressure of the industry. Getting liposuction was the fakest thing I had ever done in my career and I almost paid with my life. For the longest time I worried that the industry would replace me, but soon I realized that there will never be another me. No one looks like me, acts like me, dresses like me, or sings like me. I refused to fall for the image trap again. There are so many artists walking around depressed and medicated because they feel like they are not a hot commodity. I learned that people in this industry would do just about anything to stay relevant. I vowed that from that day forward that I would not let anyone's opinion affect me the way it did in 2004. Almost losing it all, just to be thin, was a serious wakeup call for me.

A funny thing happened to my body after my liposuction scare. I lost all the extra pounds while lying in the hospital bed on my liquid diet. A few weeks later I went back to work and promoted my second album. I was down to nearly 117 pounds and my pictures and videos were great. I continued to have a successful career and gained new fans every day. In the spring, I noticed my weight was returning. I was slowly getting bigger. With each pound I gained my smile grew wider. In July of 2004, I found out that I was pregnant with my second child, my daughter God'iss-Love. Then I truly understood my relationship with God and his sense of humor. I couldn't even be mad. God gets all the glory.

*

Chapter Eighteen

Having my second daughter, God'iss-Love, brought immeasurable joy to my heart. She was another miracle sent from the heavens. My love for my family was growing but, unfortunately, the love for my husband AL was slowly fading. Before having God'iss, our marriage had been showing signs of trouble. I was feeling abandoned more and more every day. The feeling that I once had of being protected was not there anymore. I'm not sure when the shift in our relationship began but I had a pretty good idea of why the shift occurred.

A few months before we got married, AL and I were heading out on a date. We recently had become a couple and decided to spend all of our time together. We were riding in my Mercedes Benz truck with freshly-tinted windows. AL and I had only known each other for a few months but we were as thick as thieves.

As we were cruising down the street, I noticed a car was following us for a while. I had never seen the car before and I grew concerned. When I stopped at a red light, I tried to get a good look at the person inside. All of a sudden, the vehicle pulled up alongside of us. A woman rolled down her window. Clearly, she was pissed off. She threw a red slushy beverage that smashed against the drivers' side and the window of my Mercedes.

"What the hell?" I yelled. "This bitch gotta die!"

I didn't know who the woman was and what was going on until I pulled over into a nearby police station. AL and I got out of the car and he immediately started arguing with the woman. A little boy was with her. The woman was AL's son's mother. I couldn't believe my eyes. We were only together for a few weeks and I already had to deal with a woman with a child popping into the picture. The argument caused a scene and attracted the attention of a few police officers. They asked me if I wanted to file charges.

"I want to file a restraining order," I yelled. "She just threw something on my car."

I called the record label. I was furious that I was in the middle of a domestic dispute. I didn't know if the altercation was going to escalate and make the news. I wanted to give the label a courtesy call heads up in case I was arrested. The last thing I needed was a news story to leak out that I was in the middle of a squabble in the streets.

Things did not escalate that day, but the incident shook me up. After I filed a peace order in the Anne Arundel County Circuit Court, I also purchased my first handgun, a Glock 19. I had never experienced anything like that argument with AL's ex. I had fought with females in the past and had issues with people but never to the point where I felt that my life was threatened. AL spoke about his baby's mother before we decided to become a couple, but it was clear that she would never be completely out of his life. I would soon learn that my intuition was correct. That day was far from the last time I would have to deal with their drama.

During the first year of our marriage, I felt like AL and I were truly unstoppable. Not only were we raising a family, but my career was doing very well. Between my "afternoon drive radio show" and dropping a new album, it felt like I could do anything as long as I had my happy family. I loved AL and I trusted him. When his baby's mother started creeping back into the picture, my faith in him started dissipating.

When I was younger I was taught that once I got married I was supposed to be with my husband and my family. When AL put a ring on my finger, I stopped hanging out and I spent less time with my friends. If I was not visiting with my biological family, I was home with the kids or hanging out with AL. Some days, AL wanted to hang out with his friends. He would drop me off with my family and disappear for hours. I started to become suspicious of what my husband was up to. I felt like I was being left in the dark more than I was being protected. I didn't know what my husband was getting into when he would leave me and pick me up at all hours of the night. I felt like I couldn't do the same thing that he was doing. I would never drop him off and disappear for what seemed like an eternity. After a while, I started to feel like I was trapped. They say that all things done in the dark will surely come to the light. As fate would have it, I would learn a great deal about AL's true whereabouts from his baby's mother.

While I was working at the radio station, I would get non-stop calls from AL's baby's mother. She would harass me and tell me that she was with my husband while I was at work. She would prove it to me by telling me what the inside of my car looked like on that day. She would even tell me how much loose change I had in my ashtray. The phone calls were just the start of the drama.

AL's baby's mother started sending malicious letters to my post office box. She started calling my cell phone and continued to call the station. I was beyond annoyed with the useless drama from her. I argued with AL constantly and tried to get him to handle it. She was not only affecting our marriage but she was affecting my professional career. She was out of control.

No matter how much I tried to plead with AL to protect me, his wife, from this outside threat, AL would never make it stop. My husband knew that I never wanted people to get at me. After being assaulted, I constantly felt vulnerable. The phone calls, text messages, and vicious letters had to stop. I felt disrespected knowing that she was all in our business and had access to information that no one else had. She knew my post office box number and also my cellphone number. I could only imagine what else this deranged woman knew about us. I accepted the petty drama when AL and I were just a couple. Now that we were married, all of these childish things were unacceptable.

With all the persistent phone calls and badgering, I grew tired. I started going through AL's phone and learned of other women that were contacting him. I couldn't take it anymore. I deserved better. I decided to move my daughters and me out of our family home. We went to live with my sister. For a good while, I chose to sleep on her guest bedroom floor just to get away from AL. I felt like the man who was supposed to protect me had left me more exposed than ever.

I continued to do shows to promote my album. AL

went on the road with me, but things were not the same between us. I purposely stayed away from my husband as much as I could. We tried to work on our marriage and even asked my father to counsel us. Talking to my dad helped us recognize some of our problems, but we still had a long way to go. Something had clearly changed and it was hard for us to retrieve that great chemistry we once shared. Still, AL and I eventually got back together. Despite our personal problems, we continued to handle our business and raise our daughter.

When I came home to take a break from the tours, I found myself going out more often. I was still an artist. I couldn't stop my life because I was having problems at home. When one of my girlfriends invited me to Puerto Rico, I quickly accepted. I needed a break from my home life and decided to go without my husband. I didn't ask for his permission. The vacation was just what I needed. I slept during most of the trip. The stress of the music business and my family life was clearly getting to me. I used the mini-vacation to liberate myself and relax my body.

When I returned from Puerto Rico, AL and I had a serious discussion. While I was on vacation I found out that someone had broken into my safe and had stolen nearly fifty thousand dollars cash and my pistol. I couldn't believe the news. When I asked my husband about the incident, he said he didn't know who did it. He said there had been some people at the house but no one had a clue as to how the money had gone missing. I was hurt when I found out the news. I had set the money aside for Heaven. I was saving the money to give to her on her sixteenth birthday. Now, it was gone. I was devastated, but what I would hear from my husband next would change our relationship forever.

AL eventually told me that he stole the money. He had gotten into some street trouble and needed to buy his way out of it. He immediately apologized and said that he felt bad. I couldn't believe my ears. His words hurt my heart. I walked away from AL and went into the bathroom. I cried and tried to make sense of what my husband had done. Losing the money was hurtful enough, but to know that AL did it was difficult to accept.

A few minutes later, I walked out of the bathroom and we started to talk again. I knew this was going to change our relationship, but I wanted AL to know that I forgave him. He was my husband. I was a Christian woman so I had to forgive him. AL said that he was going to return the money. He kept his word but, after that day, things would go downhill from there.

AL and I managed to stick it out for a few more years. Things were never the same between us. After the birth of my second daughter, I worked harder than ever to take care of my family. I knew that the end of my marriage was near. I had to stop allowing AL to come on the road with me because I didn't want people to believe that we were still together. The love between us was vanishing and it was just a matter of time before I walked out the door. When I did, I would never look back.

Towards the end, AL and I had a lot of conversations about our marriage. We were both honest with each other about our feelings. We knew that things had changed for a number of reasons. I'm not sure when I stopped loving AL, but somewhere along the line I started feeling like he was abandoning me. I felt like he put other people above his wife. I would never accept that. I even stepped out and found other ways to soothe my breaking heart. Although they satisfied the moment, knowing I was wrong did nothing to ease the pain. I made peace with knowing that I would never get that tingly feeling back like when he would drive to NYC to see me in the wee hours of the morning just to be by my side.

In the beginning, I believed that AL and I were like Bonnie and Clyde, inseparable. He was a quiet and semi-edgy guy and I loved that about him. He was the total opposite of the type of person that everyone believed I would marry. I thought he would protect me from anything and everything that came our way. When I felt unloved and alienated, there was no amount of sex, big hugs, or memories of our first kiss that I could muster up a desire to stay. I never wanted to be a single mommy but, at this point, single motherhood was inevitable. I was no longer in love. I had no other choice but to file for divorce.

After we separated, AL and I hated each other for a long time. It was hard for us to communicate. Things never became physical between us, but the arguments were intense. It was heartbreaking. We never argued in front of the children. It took a while but we eventually became cordial again. Our story didn't end on a good note but AL never let our troubles get in the way of visiting the girls. I'm glad we were blessed with two beautiful daughters. I wasn't perfect, but I tried my best to be a good wife. I wasn't the perfect girl, but I tried my best to be a good girl. I didn't want to allow anything that was going on in my marriage to make me change my core morals. I thank God that I was able to walk away with my daughters and start my life all over again. It hurt like all hell but I knew I would eventually heal from the pain, if not for myself then for the sake of my daughters.

Cynthia Loving

Chapter Nineteen

Queens, New York, is the birthplace of a lot of musical legends. Run-DMC, LL Cool J, Nas, Russell Simmons, Sandra "Pepa" Denton and countless others have all called Queens their home. I met dozens of rappers, singers and executives when I lived in Southside Jamaica, Queens. Back then it was common to run into an entertainer while shopping or just hanging out in one of the craziest boroughs in the city. None of those chance meetings were more important than when I met Irv Gotti.

As the founder and CEO of Murder, Inc. Records, Irv Gotti was a big name in the music industry. His record label was producing hits for a number of platinum selling artist including Jay-Z, DMX, and Aaliyah. I had heard Irv Gotti's name on a few occasions and knew that he was seriously connected in the industry. One day while I was on a video set in Queens, I got a chance to meet Irv. We discussed business. Irv had heard of me before and wanted me to write and perform on a song that he was producing for a movie soundtrack. The name of the film was "Romeo Must Die" starring Jet Li and the late Aaliyah. I agreed to do it and felt excited to collaborate on the project.

A few days later, Irv Gotti asked me to meet his artist, Dave Bing, and him at the studio. They wanted me to write the hook for a song called "Somebody Gonna Die Tonight." Irv let me hear the music and described the scene in the movie. As soon as I heard the track I knew I could come up with something great for the project. It took me about twenty minutes to write and perform the hook. Irv loved it. The song made the soundtrack and even made the movie. Irv was impressed with my vocals. He said that he was a fan of my churchy-sound and that my voice had a lot of soul to it. To show his gratitude, Irv told me that he wanted to throw me some more work in the coming weeks.

Irv Gotti was a man of his word. He called me up and told me that he wanted me to work with his top selling artist, Ja Rule. They were working on a single called "I Cry." The track featured a sample from the classic song by The O'Jays. They wanted me to add some vocals to the song. Irv played the track for me. There was another female singer on the song but Irv wanted me to replace her. Irv asked me what I thought about the record.

"Well, first of all, if that was me on the song I would've sang it on key," I jokingly said.

Everyone in the room laughed.

"Okay, that's what's up," Irv nodded his head. "So, when can you come to the studio and do your vocals?"

"Whenever y'all are ready," I replied. "We can do this today."

Irv Gotti was impressed by my confidence. A few days later they called me up to the studio. I didn't hesitate to wow them again with my vocals. Irv Gotti and the staff members at Murder, Inc. loved the record. They kept my vocals on the song and released it on Ja Rule's "Rule 3:36" album. The song started buzzing soon after the release. That record gave my career another boost.

I briefly met Ja Rule on the set of the music video for "Somebody's Gonna Die Tonight." We immediately hit it off. I was shocked by how cool he was. I enjoyed working with Irv and Ja and couldn't wait until we got to work on his project.
A few weeks later, I was back in Maryland and Ja Rule's album was doing well. He dropped the first single, "Between Me & You" featuring Christina Milian. The song was a hot but Irv was looking for another hit to compliment the first single. He called me and asked if I could get to New York to help remake a song called "Put It on Me" by Ja Rule featuring Vita. The album version didn't have any singing on it and Irv said he needed me to add my touch to it.

"Mo, I want you to get on this record," Irv Gotti said. "Can you make it to the studio in New York tonight?"

Tonight? I thought to myself. I was a four-hour-drive away from New York but there was no way I was going to miss this golden opportunity. I told him that I would be there. Irv Gotti was the type of exec that could get a song recorded and played on all of the radio stations in less than forty-eight hours. He made friends with the DJs and the program directors at the stations and reached out constantly. He knew how to get the right record into heavy rotation. I needed to bring my A-game to make this song a hit.

I arrived at the studio in New York in record time. My manager Loreal met me there and we headed inside. I felt excited to do the song but I also felt a nervous pressure come over me. I couldn't explain the intimidation I was feeling. I knew I could write and record a hit song so I tried my best to stay focused and stay confident. Irv greeted when I walked into the studio. He played the record for me and I started to vibe to the banging track.

"This is the song right here," Irv said. "The song is already on Ja Rule's album but we want you to add your flava to it."

"Alright," I responded.

I listened to the track a few more times. I heard the piano in the beginning and started to come up with a few ideas.

I turned back to Irv and said, "I need about twenty to thirty minutes. I want to add some harmony to this too. Can y'all leave the control room while I go in the booth? I'm shy. I just want it to be me and Duro."

"No problem. Anything you need," Irv said.

Everyone got up and headed outside. While Irv and the staff were in the lounge area I sat in the studio sweating bullets. I wanted to outdo myself from the "I Cry" song. I had to beat my own time and make this song was even better than the first one. I eventually calmed myself down and caught the vibe of the track. About twenty minutes later my vocals were done.

Irv and his team came back into the studio. I told him that I still needed to add some adlibs to the record but other than that the record was done. The engineer, Duro, played the track for Irv. My presence on the song was immediately felt as I started my vocals from the opening piano key.

"Where would I be...Without you baby...So if you need me....If you want me... to put it on youuuu..."

Irv listened closely to the words. The glow on his face was priceless. I could tell that he was excited about the record. The opening intro to the song continued to play through the speakers. The moment the bass dropped and Ja Rule started rapping Irv Gotti raised his arms in the air like he won The Super Bowl.

"This is a smash!" Irv yelled out in the studio. "We outta here...I knew this record was gonna be a smash hit!"

Irv's explosive response shocked me. He was yelling loudly in the studio about how the record was going to top the charts and make everyone a lot of money. I was happy that he loved the track and felt relieved that I didn't have to do a second take. I told him that I wanted to add a few more parts to the song. I stayed in the studio and recorded more vocals. I sang just behind Ja Rule's second verse and that is when the song went from being good to being a bona fide hit. *"Since we met it's been you and I... A tear for a tear, baby eye for an eye... And you know that my heart gon' cryyyy..."*

My smooth vocals complimented Ja's rough voice and the harmony we made seemed like it was destiny. Our sound meshed together like a soulful duo. Everyone in the studio could feel the energy. We were not competing with each other. We were completing each other.

Irv Gotti was visibly excited about the song. He called Lyor Cohen and the other executives from Def Jam Records into the studio. They all listened to the song and loved it. It was great watching everyone have the same reaction to it. I felt like this was going to be my breakout song and I felt blessed to be a part of the project.

"Within six weeks this song is going to be on top of the charts," Irv said, "Watch and see."

Irv Gotti wasn't lying. From the moment the song was released the response was amazing. Every Hip-Hop and R&B

radio station immediately blasted the song into heavy rotation. The fans remembered the song from Ja Rule's album but when they heard the new version they couldn't get enough of it. The vocals gave "Put It on Me" a brand new meaning and a brand new life. As the song gained momentum, we started getting flooded with requests for shows and appearances. We soon hit the road and the good times started rolling.

A few weeks later we flew down to West Palm Beach to shoot the video. Hype Williams was the director and he put together a masterpiece. I showcased my signature braids for the first time in that video. People loved the ombré style braids that started off with burgundy at the top and faded into white at the bottom. I also got the opportunity to show off my tattoos. Unlike Elektra Records, Def Jam was lenient about my hood-like style. I wore a short haircut in the "Hot Boyz" video with Missy Elliot but now I was able to introduce my new "Lil Mo" persona. In my wildest dreams I couldn't have imagined how much exposure I would receive as a result of the project.

The "Put It on Me" video took off like a rocket ship. We were touring all over the country and making appearances on major television shows. We were featured on The Jay Leno Show, Jimmy Kimmel Live, and all the music video networks. The video played on the countdown shows every day. Fans from all over the world requested the song on BET's 106 & Park Show. The song dominated the number one spot for over sixty days and "Put It on Me" became the first music video in history to get retired on the network. BET presented us with a plaque and also named it the #1 music video of 2001.

The immense love we received from the song was unlike anything I had ever felt before. Ja Rule and I grew closer while we were on the road together. We became an incredible team and even better friends. The fans could feel the energy we brought to them as a result of our bond. Whether we were in Chicago, Los Angeles, Cancun, Atlanta, New York, or DC the reception for the song was amazing. The cheers and the thunderous ovations from the crowds were taking me higher than any drug ever could. The moment people heard the first piano key they were hooked. Every show seemed to grow more intense and "Put It on Me" gave the fans four minutes and thirty-two seconds of pure bliss. I never wanted this ride to end.

The song crossed over into the mainstream and I found myself doing more shows and appearances. I started neglecting my own project but I didn't want to let this opportunity slip through my hands. "Put It on Me" quickly climbed the charts. It cracked the Billboard Top 10 and peaked at #8. The song reached #2 on the Hip-Hop and R&B Chart and #1 on the Billboard Rhythmic Top 40 Chart. The record was estimated to reach over 90 million listeners from all the radio spins. When the final number was tallied, Ja Rule's album had sold over five million units worldwide. The success of the song was mind blowing. I knew this record was going to be the song that would set me up for life. I had no clue that I was about the learn one of the hardest lessons of the music industry.

A few months after the release of "Put It on Me" I was still trying to maintain my incredibly busy schedule. I was still touring with Ja Rule and also working hard to get my own album completed. I was doing back-to-back promotional shows and traveling to every corner of the country. Murder, Inc. made sure I had a place to stay and food to eat while I was on the road, but the label was not putting money in my pocket. I was staying in plush hotels, performing in sold out arenas and even traveling on Lyor Cohen's private jet. Every day that went by I couldn't help but wonder when the money was going to come rolling in.

 One weekend while I was in Maryland I received a call to head back out on tour with Ja Rule. My manager, Loreal, was with me when an issue quickly escalated between Irv and her. I was never told the details of the disagreement but my relationship with Murder, Inc. started to change after that day. Ja Rule began to distance himself from me and my conversations with Irv Gotti were not as cordial as they once were. I had no clue what was happening behind the scenes but I could tell that something had changed.

 When we headed back out to do promotional shows the vibe between Ja Rule and me was different. Our friendship was hardening. I would perform with them and go straight to my room afterwards. I didn't make a big deal about how I was being treated. It was all about business. I honored my commitment and continued to do shows and help promote his album. Things took a turn for the worse when I didn't receive any royalty checks for "Put It on Me."

 After months of waiting for my first check, I had no choice but to act on my suspicions. I had been receiving checks for "I Cry" but I hadn't received any money for "Put It on Me." I sensed something shady was going on and I needed to get to the bottom of it. Before my vocals were recorded, Irv told me that the label had exhausted its budget for Ja Rule's project. He said the label couldn't pay me up front. My usual fee back then was $10,000 plus 10% of the writers' share. Irv informed me that the $10,000 fee was outside of the budget but said they could do the 10% royalty rate. I agreed to the deal that I thought was the verbal signature to the invisible contract.

After a few calls to the label, I found out that my paperwork was handled incorrectly. Because the original version of "Put It on Me" was already on Ja Rule's album, the label was responsible for updating the credits so that I would be included as a writer and contributor on the song. Ironically, the small miscue created a major problem for me. I was angry, hurt, and devastated by the news. I immediately pointed the blame at Irv Gotti and Ja Rule. I held them responsible for the way my paperwork was mishandled. I decided it was time to get a lawyer and sue Murder, Inc. I needed to get my money one way or another.

I eventually reached out to a high-powered attorney named Willie Gary. He was known for helping dozens of artists fight with record labels over royalty checks and owed payments. Many people referred to him as the Johnny Cochran of the music industry. Willie Gary connected me with his son, Sekou Gary. They investigated my claim against Murder, Inc. After some intense digging they came back to me with more bad news. A mountain of creditors was suing Murder, Inc. The once successful music label was in financial turmoil behind the scenes. Sekou Gary informed me that my lawsuit would be pushed to the bottom of the pile. He said there was a chance that the label would have no money left once my number was called. I decided to drop the lawsuit against Murder, Inc. I ended up taking one of the biggest financial losses of my life.

They say the worse place to be sometimes is in your feelings. And in my feelings is exactly where I was after my falling out with Murder, Inc. I was angry with Irv and Ja Rule. I felt like I was there for them when they needed me the most. I helped them make a hit record and they refused to hold up their end of the deal. I did tour dates with them and helped fuel the album while neglecting my own project. They were all riding around in expensive cars and jets. They were making boatloads of cash while I still had bills.

One day, I received a check at my house in Maryland that was meant for Ja Rule. We had the same booking agent and they mistakenly sent a check in his name worth $25,000. Ja was getting close to fifty grand a show and the check represented a deposit for an upcoming event. I contacted the booking agent and informed them of the error. They were shocked by my honesty, but Ja was my friend and I couldn't bring myself to steal from him. The check was a harsh reminder that I was still owed money from their label. My anger was too much to keep inside. I allowed the whole ordeal to affect me and I lashed out the only way I knew how.

A few weeks later I was a guest host on BET's 106 & Park show. Ja Rule was in the middle of a Hip-Hop beef with fellow Queens Rapper 50 Cent. They were making diss records about each other and the verbal confrontations were escalating. I met 50 Cent on a number of occasions when I lived in Queens. We both wrote songs at a studio belonging to a mutual friend of ours named Barry Salter. I had no problem with 50 Cent and I enjoyed his music. My intention was never to take sides during their beef but I was beyond angry with my one time friend. When the time came for me to introduce a music video by Ja Rule, I felt it was the perfect moment to take a major shot at him.

"G-G-G-G...G-Unit!" I yelled into the mic.

I knew the diss would get back to Ja Rule in a hurry but I didn't care. The quick jab was the first of many shots that I would direct at Irv Gotti and him. I didn't care how they felt about it. I would say what was on my mind. When I was a guest DJ on Hot 97 in New York I fired shots at them. I didn't consider the repercussions of my actions. I just kept taking shots and trying to embarrass them. I even released a few diss-records of my own about Ja Rule. He ultimately responded and put out a diss-record about me. People who were familiar with our close bond could not believe that we were beefing with each other. I didn't care about that bond any longer. I didn't show any signs of letting up. I was still hurt. My pride and my arrogance started to consume me. I felt that the "Put It on Me" record was nothing without me. I dared them to take me off the song. I started feeling cocky until I received a call that slowed me down.

Mona Scott from Monami Entertainment has always been a good friend of mine. We talked about anything and everything. She never hesitated to give me advice about the industry. When she got word of my problems with Ja Rule she called me up and handed me some much needed guidance.

"Mo, you are a female. Don't join in with ANY beefs." Mona said. "Sometimes those beefs are deeper than music and you don't want to be caught in the middle of that. Don't add fuel to the fire."

Mona's words stuck with me and I decided to leave it alone. Although I was still angry I realize that I could be putting myself in danger by stirring up an already boiling pot.

I stop taking shots at Murder, Inc. and eventually turned my focus back to working on my album.

Ja Rule and I eventually lost contact. As the months turned into years I started to feel differently about my old friend. I regretted how things ended between us. I allowed my unfortunate situation to make me bitter about the industry. I slowed down on doing features with other artists fearing that they were going to take my voice and not pay me for the record.

As I learned more about the music industry I realized that I was directing my anger at the wrong people. I had to accept the fact that Ja and Irv were not doing anything shady with my paperwork. It was out of their hands. I was truly on the wrong end of a mishap by the administration department. As much as I felt that Ja Rule should have fought harder for my credits to be added, I had to accept the fact that it was not his job to do so. For years, I wanted to apologize to Ja. As fate would have it, my opportunity came almost ten years after we last spoke to each other.

Around 2009, hip-hop blogs and news sites started running stories about Ja Rule's impending battle with the IRS. It was being reported that he was facing time for nonpayment of taxes along with illegal gun charges. As a fellow artist I couldn't believe people were laughing and celebrating his legal issues. I felt bad for Ja and empathized with him during his entire ordeal. Our relationship was bigger than just the "I Cry" and "Put It on Me" songs. I knew Ja's kids and his family. While everyone was pointing fingers and laughing at him, I was praying for his children. Being a child who grew up with a father that had to leave for months at a time, I knew how Ja being away could affect his family.

In 2012, Ja Rule was released after serving a two-year sentence. He was having a birthday party in New York City and I received an invitation to the event. We were working with the same publicist but, still, I was shocked once I received the invitation. I reached out to Soulgee McQueen to make sure that my invite wasn't some sort of joke or mistake.

"Mo, this is a real invite," Soulgee McQueen said. "We think this will be a great time to mend y'all relationship. This is neither for publicity nor a photo op. We all know that y'all were genuinely good friends. Y'all were cool when all the lights were flashing and y'all were flying on everybody's jets and in everybody's VIP parties. And now that he has been through some things it's time for y'all to remember where y'all started from."

I decided to go to the party. I took the four-hour drive from Maryland to celebrate with my old friend in New York. I decided to bring my security because I had no clue how Ja was going to react when he saw me. It had been over ten years since we were in the same room together. When I got to the party it was packed with people. Security quickly moved me to the VIP section and Ja was hanging out and laughing with his friends. To my surprise, Ja Rule was excited to see me.

"Mo!" Ja greeted me with open arms.

We embraced like we hadn't seen each other in a hundred years. He tried to speak but I immediately cut him off. I needed to get something off my chest first.

"What up, my nigga?" I greeted Ja. "Yo, if I ever offended you, if I ever disrespected you, whatever I did in the past, when I was younger, I apologize. I can't even be mad at you. We all live and learn. I have to apologize to you because it wasn't your fault. You didn't work the administration department for the label and that is something I had to learn. We all got burned in this industry but that was no reason to be mad at you. So I apologize for that."

Ja accepted my apology. It felt like a heavy weight was lifted off of my shoulders. It had been a long time since we talked and it felt good to be on speaking terms again. We popped a bottle and celebrated his birthday like we were still on tour together. We finally had our bond back.

A few months later I reached out to Irv Gotti on social media. I also apologized to him and congratulated him on his beautiful family. It felt good to release the useless pride that was keeping us apart. Tomorrow is not promised to any of us. I was tired of living with the burden of not expressing my regret about what happened.

I'm grateful that we are back in each other's lives, watching each other's kids grow up. That was a major part of our friendship that I missed. When Ja and I were performing on tour, we had a family bond. There was nothing sexual or scandalous about our relationship. We were great friends and the shadiness of the industry almost tore us apart.

I thank God that I got a chance to make amends with Ja and Irv. We were true friends. No matter what happens between friends, if the bond is real there nothing that can tear it apart. No one made me drive four hours away just to apologize to someone I hadn't seen in ten years. Only God could do that. Only God could put me in a situation to go back, apologize, pick up where we left off, and move forward. I'm so happy that I obeyed when the opportunity presented itself. I thank God for the blessing of true friends with unbreakable bonds.

Chapter Twenty

Since the day I started to make a name for myself in the music game, I made it my business to avoid the temptation of dating anyone from the industry. Being on tour with countless acts opened my eyes to a very ugly side of the music world. Committed men frequently cheated on their girlfriends and their wives while they were out on the road. I never wanted to be the woman who found herself dealing with lies and infidelity. Early in my career, I made up my mind that I would never get involved with anyone who would put me through that type of drama, but, in 2005, a man who would make me break my very own rule about dating industry men entered my life.

Darnell Jackson was a rising star in the music world. His sensual R&B sound was breathtaking and fans across the country loved his music. We had met on a number of occasions while we were performing on the road. Our relationship started as passing friends. Our careers were heading down a similar path and we often found ourselves performing on the same stage. He was always polite and professional and for the longest time I considered Darnell to be just a co-worker. Later that year we were booked on the same tour. That is when our relationship began to grow deeper.

    Back home, my personal life was slowly deteriorating. Despite the industry success I was having on the tour, I was fighting a losing battle on the home front. I was in the process of ending my marriage. It was just a matter of time before I would be divorced. This was the second time that I was separated from my husband. There was no chance that we were going to be a happy family again. Our second separation was the final straw.

    Darnell grabbed my attention at just the right time. I was going through a lot of turmoil with my divorce. Between the baby-mama-drama and the constant red flags in my prior relationship, I was beyond ready for a change. I didn't want to date any random guys while I was on tour. I considered Darnell to be a friend and we enjoyed each other's company in between shows. Hanging out with Darnell made me happy. He started to show me that there was life outside of my failed marriage. I was attracted to Darnell's affectionate side. He was also very thoughtful. Darnell sent gifts to my tour bus in between shows. Those small gestures always kept a smile on my face. During a time when I didn't want to be *Lil' Mo* every day, Darnell made me feel like the girl I wanted to be. After a few months of dating, Darnell and I went from being "tour friends" to being "best friends."

    Being in a relationship with an R&B singer was thrilling. Darnell Jackson was notorious for making women throw their panties on stage for him. His sensual vocals drove women crazy. I always felt a rush knowing that all of his female fans wanted him badly but that from the moment he left the stage I was the woman he was with. It was the perfect relationship for me. Darnell and I had similar situations at the time. He and I were both going through nasty breakups and looking to rebound from the drama at home. We both had kids of our own and shared a love for family. He adored and respected my parents and the feelings were reciprocated. My family embraced him and we spent a lot of great times together.

The chemistry we shared also spilled over into our professional careers. I performed with him and was even featured in one of Darnell's music videos. After a while there was no denying the path we were on. We were best friends who shared our deepest secrets with each other. We were both recording artists who shared a bond that was hard to break. Despite the fact that we were unprepared to start a new relationship we decided to make it official and become a couple. I swore off industry men but there was something about Darnell that I could trust. He was far from the thug type and his sensual side attracted me. He was a true gentleman and never missed an opportunity to show me how much he cared about me.

One evening while Darnell was at an event, his phone mistakenly dialed me. I picked up the phone expecting to speak to my new boyfriend but all I could hear was a lot of commotion. Darnell's voice was loud in the background. He was yelling at someone and my name continued to surface. I later learned that someone was attempting to disrespect me when I wasn't around and Darnell immediately checked the person. His willingness to defend me made me fall for him even harder. Shielding and protecting me has always been a must for any man seeking my heart. Darnell was the type of person who loved hard. I admired that about him. He was definitely the man I needed in my life at the time.

In the fall of 2005, Hurricane Katrina ripped through the Gulf Coast. Our tour was cut short and Darnell and I headed back home. We both lived in Maryland at the time and decided to continue our relationship. Out of respect for each other's privacy, we kept our relationship out of the watchful eye of the media. We didn't want everyone in our business and refused to allow the press to destroy what we had built together. The emotional connection we shared was strong. We both were highly committed and everyone around us could tell that we were in love. Still, after ten months our relationship began to shift. Our hectic schedules clashed and Darnell and I spent less time together. The combination of long studio hours and sold-out shows kept us apart from one another. The absence began to take its toll. Despite seeing less of each other I never felt that our relationship was in jeopardy. A few months later, I received a text message that would crush me like never before.

By the middle of 2006, Darnell Jackson found himself back on the road and doing a lot of performances. He called me one day and told me that he was heading back to Maryland and wanted to get together. I was excited to see him again and asked him to reach out to me once he was back in town. That particular day was extremely busy for me but I was looking forward to catching up with him. My youngest daughter God'iss Love was sick that day. Most of my morning was spent tending to her. I was away from my phone for most of the day and never realized that Darnell was reaching out to me. By the time I got to my phone I noticed a number of missed calls from him. I immediately called him back but he never picked up the phone. After a few hours I tried him again but he refused to take my call. I sent Darnell a text message and asked him if everything was okay. After a few minutes he responded. His reply made my jaw drop to the floor.

"I'm breaking up with you because I can't get you on the phone," Darnell texted me.

The strange message stopped me in my tracks. I stared at it for a few minutes. I couldn't believe what I was reading. I texted him to make sure that I was reading the words correctly. For a moment, I thought someone had stolen his phone. I even thought he was trying to play a joke on me. After a short discussion, Darnell told me how he felt and made it clear that our relationship was coming to an abrupt end. The news broke my heart. I was looking forward to building something special with Darnell but it was evident that our time was over.

"Are you sure this is something you want to do?" I asked Darnell. "Make sure that you are sure."

Darnell never backed away from his decision. He was adamant about the break up. I had to accept the tough reality that it was time for me to move on. Flashbacks of my first divorce started to hit me and now I was going through a rough break up with my boyfriend. We never had any major problems in our relationship. Like any other young couple, we would have disagreements but we always made it a point to work out our problems before the end of the day. Darnell's text message left me with a boatload of questions. I never understood why he broke up with me. I thought we both were happy. I never noticed any signs of trouble before that infamous text message. For the longest time I blamed myself, but I was clueless as to what I had done to make him turn away from me.

Out of respect for our bond, Darnell and I continued to be friends. We stayed in contact and encouraged one another as we navigated through our careers. A few years later we had a chance to reconnect. We talked about our relationship and how it ended.

"You know you broke my heart, right?" I said to Darnell during one of our conversations.

"I didn't break your heart," Darnell replied. "I actually spared it."

Darnell's response made me look at our breakup in a different light. In typical Darnell fashion, I learned that he was again looking out for my best interest. Building something with Darnell helped me to move on and avoid staying in the toxic relationship that was my first marriage. Darnell went on to tell me that he believed that he couldn't give me everything that I needed in a relationship. He said I deserved more than what he could offer. We both were dealing with a lot back then and the timing of our relationship eventually was our downfall. We were best friends and we shared a great connection. Looking back, we both can honestly say that we were not ready for each other. We pushed the envelope and ruined a good thing by becoming a couple. Darnell and I never wanted to believe that we were each other's rebound situation but time proved us both wrong.

Darnell and I eventually moved on. In 2007, about a year after our breakup, I found myself entering into a new relationship with the man who would become my second husband. Darnell and I continue to be good friends and we never lost contact. He still looks out for me and never hesitates to share his connections to help push my career forward. From checking up on me to giving me advice about the business, Darnell always stays true to his friendly bond and never crosses the line. He respects me completely and never does anything to disrupt my personal life. His mom is still cool with my family and the love will always be there between us. Darnell once said that I was the one that got away. Despite the breakup, there is nothing negative I could say about Darnell Jackson. We had a great time together and we were truly best friends. We still joke about the fact that he broke up with me via text message. Although it hurt immensely at the time, we can still get a good laugh out of it.

I learned a lot about myself from the time I spent with Darnell. I learned that getting a divorce was not the end of the world. I also learned that there was always somebody out there who would love me for me, even if the love doesn't last forever. Darnell and I were hopeless romantics. We were both coming out of bad situations when we started dating. Looking back, it was evident that we should have waited to start a new relationship. Having some time to be alone and to learn more about ourselves was probably the best thing to do at the time. There are moments in each of our lives when it is okay to be single and to love ourselves. Nevertheless, I enjoyed everything about my relationship with Darnell Jackson. Even knowing what I know today, I wouldn't do anything differently. Darnell was worth all of the heartache and every gut-wrenching moment of our break up. It was no coincidence that Darnell was the one man that made me break my life long rule about dating industry men, but that is one rule that I would smash into a thousand pieces if I had to do it all over again.

*

Cynthia Loving

PART IV

P.S. I Love Me

Chapter Twenty-One

A few months after breaking up with Darnell Jackson, I started reevaluating my choice in men. I had dated a bad boy, a rapper, an R&B star, and even a gun-toting criminal. Everyone that I had allowed into my life was far removed from the values that I learned in church as a little girl. The men that I was sharing my love, my body, and my soul with were damaging me from the inside out. I could never blame my exes for the love lost. It was up to me to use better judgment when choosing the man in my life. I still desired to have a family and to be happily in love. The following year, I would regain my confidence and muster up the strength to, once again, give love a try.

It was Mother's Day in 2007 and I was wrapping up a performance at a church in North Carolina. At the time, I was working with a record company called Drakeweb Music Group. The company asked me to help an artist who needed a ride from North Carolina to Maryland. He was a gospel singer on the same label and he needed to take the five-hour trek for a studio appointment the next day. I had plenty of room in my van and didn't mind doing the favor.

A few hours later, my team and I were waiting for the gospel singer. There was heavy rain in the forecast and we were all itching to leave. We all had things to do in Maryland and I was anxious to get home to my daughters. The last place I wanted to be was in North Carolina stranded in a passing storm.

A few minutes later, the gospel singer showed up. I had never seen him before so we introduced ourselves. His name was PJB. There was something special about him. PJB was polite and sweet. I could tell that he was from the church. He thanked us for waiting and then we headed up to Maryland. We didn't have much of a conversation that day. Everyone was exhausted. Outside of a few words, the ride was relatively quiet.

The next day, I was in the studio finishing up a song. I was mixing down one of the tracks for my upcoming album and PJB was in another studio session recording. Someone from the label suggested that PJB and I should work together. I was initially skeptical about the idea because I had never heard him sing before. When someone in the studio played one of his tracks, I was blown away by his vocals. I was impressed by his sound. He was also gifted on the keys.

"Wow, you can really sing," I complimented him.

"Thanks," PJB responded. "So, can I get you on a song?"

I had never worked with him before but I was willing to give it a shot. He played the track for me and immediately created my part to the song. I was pressed for time so I couldn't stick around. I recorded my vocals but didn't stay to hear the finished product. I made my way to the exit.

PJB noticed that I left my shawl. He tried to get my

attention to give it back to me but my road manager stopped him. I was still shielded and paranoid from being attacked back in 2001. My road manager never allowed too many people to get close to me. We never wanted a repeat of the assault in San Francisco, so everyone around me was always on guard. I was unaware that PJB was trying to get my attention before I left the studio that day.

A few weeks later, I was in New York City visiting with my music label. We were discussing the details of releasing my new album "Pain & Paper." After our meeting was over, the topic of PJB and the song we recorded surfaced. My manager called up PJB and put me on the phone. PJB wanted me to hear the track so he played it over the phone. It sounded amazing. I could feel our chemistry. We talked for a while about the song and PJB coolly switched the subject. He remembered that he couldn't get my attention back in the studio and he was not going to make the same mistake twice.

"Let's exchange numbers so we can keep in touch," PJB said.

"Okay, cool," I responded. "Send me a text so I can have your number, too."

PJB intrigued me. He was a nice guy, a sweetheart. He was the complete opposite of the men from my past. He wasn't a thug or a bad boy. He had an edge to him but he was very funny. He always kept me laughing. As a gospel artist, he was bred with a spirituality that I was drawn to. He was clearly the change I needed in my life. Our chemistry made me feel like I was moving in the right direction.

Later that month, PJB and I had a discussion. My former music director took on another job with R&B artist Carl Thomas. I was looking for someone to replace him. My band members were very good but I knew I could get a better sound out of them. PJB agreed to take the job. Within the first week of taking over the band, PJB had worked his magic. He whipped them into shape and they created an amazing sound. His incredible talent and musical gifts blew me away again. The band started doing shows with me. PJB and I became closer.

In July of 2007, I was slated to open for Patti LaBelle at a concert in Baltimore. It was a very hot day but I was looking forward to another great performance. I invited my entire family. I couldn't wait to showcase the new music from the upcoming album. This would be the first major event that I would do with the new band members.

The show was a success. PJB gave the band a five-star sound. The crowd enjoyed my show and my family had a great time. We all gathered back stage and congratulated each other on another great performance. We remained in the VIP area and waited for Patti LaBelle to perform. While I was talking to my family, I noticed that PJB had walked away. He was on the phone. Something was wrong. I grew concerned and walked up to PJB. The look on his face was disturbing. My dad went to talk to him.

"Is everything okay?" I asked.

"That was his ex-wife's mother on the phone," my dad said. "PJB's son just passed away."

"Oh, my God!" I gasped.

My world just stopped. Nothing else around us mattered. The shattering news froze me. PJB was devastated. The phone call had consumed him to the point where he was speechless. I felt deeply empathetic for my new friend. I just wanted to be there for him. PJB had learned that his eighteen-month old son was playing with a toy ball and had swallowed it. No one in the house could save him. His son died from asphyxiation.

There are no words one could use to console a person who has lost a young child. I did everything I could to be there for PJB. We were just friends that day but I felt a profound connection with him. I realized he would need everyone around him to be there for support and I was no exception.

After that sad summer day, PJB and I started spending a lot of time together and gradually grew closer. Our relationship began to build and we became more than friends. During the most difficult time of his life, we found something special between us. We became inseparable. We grew from friends to lovers within a few months. We never wanted to be away from each other.

A year to the day that PJB received the worst news of his life, we exchanged vows. The joy and pain we shared together was too intense to ignore. This was the beginning of a new chapter in our lives. On July 7, 2008, we were pronounced man and wife and were also expecting a son. The timing was perfect. God had blessed us with a 9 pound baby and on January 16, 2009, Justin McKenzie Phillip Bryant was brought into this world.

*

Cynthia Loving

Chapter Twenty-Two

The first two years of my marriage with PJB was everything that I wanted at the time. After my ugly divorce, I was nervous about taking the big plunge again, but being with PJB made me want to be a wife again. He was different from what I was used to. We were on our way to building something special together. PJB was my manager, my husband, and my best friend. Because he was a musician, it was easy for me to invite him out to my shows to handle my sound. With my DJ playing the track and PJB playing the keys, the arrangement seemed perfect. Working and traveling together only added more joy to our union. The great music we made together made me feel like we were going to be together forever.

Before we were married, my relationship with PJB was exciting. Our chemistry made it easy for us to mix business and pleasure, but after a few years of marriage our relationship seemed to change. As my manager and music director, PJB gained a lot of control over my career. The people that I trusted and worked with started to be replaced with new faces. PJB would fire anyone who disagreed with him. Despite the constant change around me, I rarely questioned PJB's motives. I learned from an early age that a good wife is submissive and obedient. I trusted PJB. I believed that my husband knew what was best for me. I allowed PJB to make a lot of my career decisions until I started to feel like he was trying to take over my life.

To reenergize my career, I started searching for a new sound. My constant networking eventually led me to a great producer named Teddy Riley. He did amazing work for everyone in the business, from Michael Jackson to Jay-Z and to Lady Gaga. I worked with Teddy Riley for a while and I loved the music we created together. I went to PJB and suggested that Teddy Riley should be the executive producer for my new album. To my surprise, my suggestion caused issues.

"Well, if you think he can give you the sound you are looking for then you should go ahead and work with him," PJB snapped at me.

PJB eventually quit as my music director and produced fewer songs for me. I didn't understand why PJB didn't support my decision. I felt like my project was not being taken seriously. I needed to make a change.

PJB started doing sessions with countless artists and I was never invited. He insisted on going out on tour with me but when I was rarely asked to accompany him to work on his projects. I even financed trips to the West Coast with an entire team of people, but I was not invited. I started to feel shut out. There was something changing between us and I didn't like it. In the beginning of our relationship, I felt like I was under PJB's leadership. Our relationship took a turn for the worse when I felt like I was being controlled and abandoned.

I was not only feeling abandoned when it came to my music but also in the bedroom. The sex in our marriage quickly became routine. The lust and passion in our sex life was fading away. There was no affection or attention. Most nights we would just have loveless sex, wash up, and go to sleep. I didn't feel the love. Being taken for granted by my husband began to take a toll on our relationship.

"We gotta get this money," PJB would always say to me when I would tell him how I felt.

There is more to a marriage then trying to get money. I am a girl. When I'm in a relationship, I hate feeling abandoned. I love for a man to make me feel that he wants me to be happy. Open my car door, make me a plate of food, help me clean house, or take out the trash. Do something that shows me that I'm in a relationship, not by myself.

After a number of years the marriage started causing me stress. The marital problems were then compounded with financial problems. Bill collectors started freezing my accounts and the IRS came after me. My world seemed to be spinning out of control. The stress and anxiety consumed me. I fell into a state of depression. Stress pains, nosebleeds and migraines were a daily occurrence. Some days, I even contemplated suicide. When I turned to my husband for support, my cries were met with coldness.

"You gotta get yourself together," my husband would say to me.

The normal support from a loving spouse was absent. I have always been a trooper so I tried my best to put things back in order. Soon I learned that my body could handle only a limited amount of stress.

One day, I was driving and feeling stressed. My financial problems, work problems, and marital issues weighed heavily on my mind. My vision became blurry. I grew nervous as my body was going through changes. I pulled over to the side of the road. I was scared and didn't know what to do, so I called my husband.

"I need you to come get me," I nervously said. "I don't know what's going on. My body feels like it's shutting down and my eyes are blurry."

"Well, what do you want me to do?" PJB raised his voice at me. "I'm all the way at the house right now. I can't get no ride out there."

PJB's anger surprised me. I immediately called my dad and told him that I was in trouble. A few minutes later, I couldn't feel most of my body. I was shutting down. I couldn't use my hands at all and I could barely speak. Thank God my father answered my call. He stayed on the phone and called 911 for me. My iPhone had an app called LocateMyPhone on it so the ambulance was able to find my car on I-95 North. I had no use of my hands. I struggled to unlock the door with my elbow. The paramedics eventually pulled me out of the car and rushed me to the hospital.

I found out why my body had shut down on me. All of my levels were very low including my oxygen, potassium, and my iron. The anxiety had pushed me over the edge.

"I can't do this anymore," I thought to myself. My marriage was draining me and I needed to make a change. In addition to feeling alone and abandoned, I started getting clues that PJB was possibly being disloyal. Text messages and emails were popping up from different women.

The messages only added to my stress. In 2011, I couldn't take it anymore. I left PJB and moved to my parents' house. I didn't trust him and my heart was broken.

News of our separation and impending divorce shocked everyone. My family was there to support me and I was grateful for their love. People from the church heard about our separation. PJB's pastor offered to pay for our counseling. I initially rejected the idea. The pastor suggested we speak to a counselor who was unfamiliar with us so that we could get an unbiased opinion about our situation. I eventually agreed to the counseling. We were scheduled to do six sessions.

During our first session, PJB and I barely looked at each other. The love between us had been compromised and it was evident in our body language. During the second session, PJB and I began to break the ice. We started warming up to each other and promised that we both would try to make changes. During the third session, PJB and I were laughing and joking with each other like we were newlyweds. We had been working on our marriage and spending more time together. Later that year, I found out that I was pregnant. After our third session, we stopped going to counseling. We promised to make changes and make a better home. On July 10, 2012, we welcomed the arrival of our second beautiful son, Jonah Maddox-Phillip Bryant.

Despite the joy we shared of having our second son, the festering issues in our marriage began to surface again. Our relationship spiraled in a freefall. I didn't want our troubles to make the headlines so we did our best to keep our issues out of the public's eye. I was still performing and doing shows and PJB continued to accompany me. We kept up appearances for the cameras, but behind closed doors we were like enemies. The relationship was becoming more toxic by the day. Despite the troubles, we continued to make an attempt to breathe life back into our dying union.

One day PJB approached me about an idea. We were not having a lot of sex in our marriage and PJB thought of a way to spice things up for us. While we were relaxing at home he called up a friend from his church. She was a member of his praise and worship team and she was also a one-time background singer for me. They talked for a few minutes and then PJB turned on his camera phone. They started speaking on FaceTime and the conversation turned sexual.

"Watch what I can make her do," PJB said.

I was shocked when the background singer started undressing for my husband. A red flag immediately went off in my head but I didn't stop the show. PJB told her to get completely naked for us. I grew very suspicious when she complied with no hesitation. PJB and the background singer were very comfortable with the sexual conversation. I was too drunk and high off medication to protest. I went along with PJB's plan and was curious to see where this would lead.

PJB and I called the background singer on a few occasions. The sexual conversations escalated and PJB decided it was time to invite her over to have a threesome. The background singer agreed to join us. Although my husband and I were not virgins, when it came to threesomes I was concerned about inviting a longtime friend into our bedroom. Despite my reservations I went along with the plan. A few weeks later, PJB decided to have a small party at our house after church. He invited a few members from his congregation over to our house including the background singer. We often had drinking parties and played games at our home when the kids were not around, but something was different about this particular evening. Everyone was drinking heavily and having a great time. The rules of the drinking game were simple. Our friends would drink until they passed out. Wherever they passed out is where they would stay for the rest of the night. Some of them would stay in our living room, some in the basement, and some even stayed in our garage. People were drinking so much that evening that it didn't take long for things to get out of control.

In the middle of the game, the background singer started acting very weird. She drank an entire cup of liquor straight and fell out of her chair. She put her face down on the floor and put her ass in the air. The background singer started screaming on the kitchen floor.

"Where's PJB?" The girl laughed out loud and yelled again, "Where's PJB?"

PJB was upstairs. Everyone in the kitchen started laughing. I was nearly drunk too, but I was sober enough to feel uncomfortable about this girl yelling for my husband with her ass in the air. She got up off the floor and everyone continued partying.

About an hour later, the party started winding down. A few of our friends already had passed out for the evening. I never wanted to leave liquor bottles lying around my house so I started cleaning up. I was looking for the background singer. She was not in the kitchen or in the living room. I walked upstairs to the second floor. I noticed two guys from PJB's production crew were upstairs. They were laughing as they walked out of my and. I immediately headed inside. The background singer was in my room. She was alone. I couldn't figure out why she was so comfortable with being in my room or why she seemed to know her way around my home. A few minutes later, PJB walked into the bedroom and closed the door. I tried to act like I didn't know what was going on but I knew what was going down.

Not long after the three of us were alone things quickly turned sexual. I participated as much as I could but it was hard for me to enjoy myself. My body was numb from the alcohol and the painkillers. I had been self-medicating the entire evening just to make it through the experience. The background singer was handling both of us with no problem. She was clearly enjoying herself. I couldn't help but feel suspicious about why my husband and she were so comfortable with each other. There was no love left in my marriage so I didn't interrupt their fun. It would be just a matter of time before I left PJB and moved on with my life. Even as I was in the middle of the threesome with my soon-to-be ex-husband, I wanted to see just how far they would take things.

"Why don't y'all kiss?" I said and motioned to PJB.

Without hesitation, the background singer and PJB started kissing right in front of me. A few minutes later, the background singer was on all fours on my bed. I couldn't believe my eyes when I watched PJB get behind this girl and start having sex with her right in front of me. The girl barely flinched when he entered her. Watching them made me even more wary.

When a woman gets a new sexual partner, her body naturally reacts to him whether he is larger or smaller than her previous partner. When the background singer and PJB started having sex, I didn't see her react at all. I realized that this wasn't their first time.

After that, I knew that there was no way I could trust PJB ever again. My heart was completely out of the marriage. My trust was gone. Everyone in the house wanted to know what happened in our bedroom that evening but we never said a word. PJB told everyone that the background singer had gotten sick and fell asleep in our room. I never got any proof that PJB and the background singer were having an affair before that evening. PJB denied it every time I approached him about it. I never trusted his excuses and I believe deep in my heart that PJB invited her into our bedroom to cover up their fucking mess.

A few months later, I separated from PJB. Our relationship deteriorated more each day as I waited for our divorce to be final. In the state of Maryland, a couple has to wait one full year before a divorce is granted. I had left PJB once before but I knew this time would be different. My life was changing fast and we were headed down two different paths. The stress and anxiety in my life needed to be lifted. PJB and I both knew that our marriage had run its course. I wanted out more than I wanted to be alive.

*

Cynthia Loving

Chapter Twenty-Three

In December of 2012, I received a call about a new television show called R&B Divas: LA. Think Factory Media, the production company for the show, was searching for six dynamic divas to star in the new reality series. I was floored by the news that I was selected to be one of the divas for the show. I would be co-starring alongside Michel'le, Kelly Price, Dawn Robinson, Chante Moore, and Claudette Ortiz. I had been searching for an opportunity to get my career back on track. The reality show would be just the boost I needed. Although my marriage was in shambles and my personal life was a mess, I never lost my spunk or my tenacity. A few industry friends and close associates tried to convince me not to do the show but I put my decision in the hands of God and trusted that He knew what was best.

A month later, I packed up my sons and moved to Los Angeles to begin taping the first season. My daughters stayed with my parents to finish out the school year. PJB and I were separated at the time. In order to keep up appearances, PJB traveled to the West Coast with me.

When we arrived in Los Angeles, I knew that it was going to be an amazing experience. The other divas and I met with Think Factory the day before we started filming the first season. They outlined our production schedule. The company explained that R&B Divas: LA would be different from a lot of reality shows. Although drama and disagreements were to be expected, there would be no fighting or physical altercations on the show. They also informed us that our homes would be the set for most of the tapings. I have always been a fan of reality television so getting a glimpse of how things worked on the set was cool.

"Because all of the divas have unique stories, we will show you guys how it all comes together," One of the producers explained during our meeting, "Please know that this will get tough at times and you guys will probably hate us at one point, but please trust the process. It is all for your benefit in the end."

I had worked with Chante Moore before. Kelly Price also was a good friend of mine. I attended her church when I was in LA. Her pastor, Shep Crawford, is a great writer who penned one of my first singles, "Ta-Da," in 1999. It felt good to have a friend on the show. Before I got the call to join the cast, Kelly and I had been discussing the opportunity. We made a pact that if we both were selected for the series, we would tell our stories the way that we wanted them to be told.

The first two weeks of production was a thrill. It was exciting working with the other divas. The production company had a great season lined up for us. It was going to be a lot of work but also a lot of fun. All of the ladies were asked to bring their A-game to make this series a success. I was up for the challenge. After a few weeks of smooth sailing, things become rocky. A couple of the divas began to show up late for filming and tensions began to mount. When it came to the entertainment industry, I was always taught to arrive early for everything. Arriving early showed people that you were serious. To arrive on time was being late. Showing up late demonstrated that you had no respect for everyone else's time.

The offense was compounded by the visible lack of interest. Some of the ladies appeared disinterested and frustrated to be on the set. They took the term "diva" a bit too far and started behaving badly towards the staff and the production company. When I started receiving the same shady treatment from some of the divas, things exploded.

Kelly Price and I had been friends for a long time. I consider Kelly to be my big sister in the industry. During the filming of the show we had a few disagreements that led to Kelly not speaking to me. I was shocked when Kelly had no words for me. I took it personally. I spoke to the production company about the issue. They suggested that I set up a scene with Kelly to try to resolve our differences. A few days earlier, Kelly had quit "The Divalogues," which was the climax project of our show. "The Divalogues" was an opportunity for us to tell the world our deepest secrets and to divulge the trials that we had to overcome in our lives. I was going to try to convince her to continue with the project.

Production set up the scene between Kelly and me and it was time for us to speak. Nothing went as planned. Our discussion quickly turned sour and we started to argue. I tried to explain to Kelly that I had reached out to her several times. I sent her text messages and called her, but she never responded. I was hoping that our meeting could be an opportunity for us to clear the air. I wanted Kelly to reconsider coming back to the show and to do "The Divalogues."

"I'm not going to have this discussion here!" Kelly snapped at me.

She became abrasive with me and I immediately became defensive. The scene turned ugly and Kelly walked off the set. I was extremely angry with her. I thought our friendship was stronger than a petty disagreement. I was wrong.

When Kelly left the show, the media got wind of the rift. During the airing of the first season there were a lot of rumors swirling around about the drama. Our issues started to play out in the public during interviews. Kelly and I took verbal shots at each other. My feelings were hurt and I didn't mind talking about our beef to the media. I knew I was wrong for continuously blasting my friend, but my feelings were hurt. Kelly and I spent an entire year without speaking to each other. That would all change when I received a call from a mutual friend.

Hip-Hop artist and longtime friend, Foxy Brown, is no stranger to industry drama. She was involved with a rift with fellow Hip-Hop artist Lil' Kim. The drama between the two female rappers played out in the magazines, the Hip-Hop blogs, and even in a few records. Foxy Brown and Kelly Price are also good friends. Foxy Brown called me one evening and we spoke about my issue with Kelly.

"Now, Mo, you know you are my baby," Foxy Brown said. "I don't want to get involved with anything if you don't want me to, but Kelly hit me up and asked me if I still had your number. She said she wants to hash out this situation."

The timing of Foxy's phone call was perfect. Kelly had been on my mind since we stopped speaking. I was waiting for an opportunity to fix what was broken between us.

"You know, Mo, I have read all of the stuff in the blogs and I just knew this couldn't be true," Foxy said. "I know how the media likes to hype things up. We all know how this industry is. I just knew you guys would have hashed this out by now."

Foxy offered to call Kelly up and connect both of us. She said she wouldn't interfere with our conversation. She would just let us talk our issues out. I agreed to the call. I wanted to let Kelly know how I felt. I waited on the other line as Foxy called Kelly. As soon as I heard my friend's voice, I started the conversation.

"Let me start off by saying that I apologize," I said to Kelly. "I apologize for anything you heard me say or anything I did in those interviews and anything I said on the show. I didn't mean to personally attack you. I just want you to know that I love you and that I respect you."

Kelly and I talked for a few and we apologized to each other. It felt good to have my good friend back in my life. I felt like an enormous weight was lifted off of me when we spoke that evening. I had been harboring very ill feelings about Kelly. As a Christian woman, it wasn't right for me to be fighting with my sister. Kelly and I have cried together and shared some of our darkest secrets with each other. I never would have imagined that a simple misunderstanding on a reality show could jeopardize our friendship.

Kelly ended up leaving R&B Divas: LA but we remain cordial. Despite the drama with my friend, I have never regretted my decision to join the cast of the reality series. The doors that have opened up as a result and the exposure that has affected my life and career are immeasurable. The show has been a tremendous blessing to my family and me.

In 2014, I returned for another season of R&B Divas: LA. My career has continued to change for the better. Still, despite the strides I was making in my professional life, my personal life was still in shambles and before I could find peace, I first had to go through 30 days of hell.

*

Chapter Twenty-Four

R&B Divas: LA has been seen by millions of people. Countless fans around the world have tuned in week after week and have seen my life play out in the public arena. They have witnessed my joy, my pain, my flaws, my ups and my downs. During production of the second season, my personal life was going through a major change. My second husband and I were waiting for our divorce to be finalized. The process drained me emotionally. I moved back to Los Angeles and got ready to film the show. I informed the production company that PJB would not be joining me to tape the second season. My story was going to change and I would take this journey alone. I didn't know how the public would receive the news of my divorce. The previous season featured PJB and me as a married couple, but behind the scenes we were barely talking to one another. I was ready to reveal the truth to the world. I needed to break free.

During the first couple of weeks of production, my emotions were running high. I had to fight back the stress that weighed heavy on my mind. Some days, I would return home after filming, sit alone, and cry. I was drinking a lot of liquor and taking pain pills. The transition was a lot to deal with, but for the sake of my kids and my family I had to muster up the strength to make it through.

PJB had returned to Maryland and we were barely communicating. Our divorce was only a few months from being finalized. Despite our differences, I could have never imagined that our separation and impending divorce would turn ugly.

On March 8, 2014, we wrapped production of the second season of R&B Divas: LA. I returned to Maryland the next day. My children had returned a month before me. I thought all would be well when I landed. Earlier that week, my father texted to inform me that PJB had picked up the remote for my garage. PJB said he needed to pick up some final things from my home. I thought he was completely moved out. My sister told me he moved into his apartment nearly a month earlier. I was clueless as to why he needed to get into my home again.

When I got home, I was hit with a harsh dose of reality. My basement door had been kicked in. Countless items were missing from my home. My music studio was emptied and the only remaining items were a few chairs and broken glass. I walked around the house and noticed more items that were missing. When I went into my master bedroom, I panicked. My fifty-five inch television was gone. I called the police believing that I was a victim of a robbery. I couldn't believe my eyes. I walked into the basement and noticed the mildew stench which led me to believe there had been a flood. I grew angrier by the minute. When the police arrived they asked me if I had any idea who might have created the damage and taken the items. I informed them that my estranged husband was the only person with access to the premises while I was away. I was told that I couldn't press charges because of the state law. I was left to deal with the damage on my own. I was devastated.

In the coming days, more issues surfaced. I was left with a four-thousand dollar light bill. My water was off due to an issue with the well line and sump pump. And after calling an insurance adjuster I learned that a dangerous mold problem was getting worse by the day. It was too dangerous to live in my home. My children and I were forced to live between my parents' house and hotels for the next thirty days. It was pure hell.

Within days, I started getting information from mutual friends about what had happened to my home. PJB's social media posts also caused me to believe that he was responsible. We never came to a resolution, but I had to be strong and move on. My family and friends got behind me and helped me get my home back in order. Watching my children live out of their suitcases for the next thirty days was tough for me. I was furious, hurt, and confused. I cried for weeks wondering when this nightmare would end.

It's been said that troubles and heartaches carry with them the seed of an equal or greater benefit. Because of the water damage to my home I was forced to part ways with a lot of my belongings. I tossed boxes of things that I was harboring from my past. I trashed everything from workout equipment to old furniture. After a few days of purging, I decided to throw away all of the useless clutter from my past. After twelve years of being a slave to two marriages, I had accumulated a lot of things. I wanted to get rid of everything that reminded me of my two failed marriages. I began to feel better with each item that I threw away. I tossed old pictures, clothes, and piles of paper. When I turned my attention to my master bedroom, I decided to get rid of my mattresses. It was the same mattress from the night of the threesome. I needed to move on and put that chapter of my life behind me. When my old mattress was removed from the house, it felt like a spirit was lifted. When I came back from Los Angeles, I had been dreading going home. After I removed the old energy from my house, things changed.

My children and I eventually moved back into our estate home. As always, my family was there to support me through my thirty days of hell. My divorce had since been finalized and I was free to love again. The emotional baggage created by my second marriage almost caused me to give up. There were even times when I almost lost my family because of the drama that my marriage created. Words could never describe the inner peace I feel with my family is back in my life. Cynthia Bryant is no longer with us. I had to remove myself from the toxic relationship. For the sake of my sanity, my happiness, and my family it was time to move my loving spirit into a better place. Finally, Cynthia Loving is back.

Chapter Twenty-Five

"Are you ready?" A text message flashed on the screen of my phone.

"Who this?" I curiously responded.

"This is Karl Dargan. Are you ready for me?"

The text messages surprised me. The irony of the question made my heart flutter. The timing seemed to be perfect. I was conversing with a young man I had met nearly ten years ago. We had crossed paths in Philadelphia at an event called Powerhouse. He had introduced himself as Karl "Dynamite" Dargan. He was a professional boxer. KD was not shy about letting me know that he was interested in me. I was happily married at the time and had just given birth to my first daughter. KD respected the fact that I was a married woman. We had a brief conversation and went our separate ways.

KD and I had reconnected years later, but we kept everything open and fun on social media. As the problems in my second marriage started mounting, I turned to my Twitter page to vent on a number of occasions. KD noticed that things were shaky on my home front so he started checking in on me. We stayed in contact this time around. KD and I eventually became good friends. By the time we reconnected, we both had gone through numerous failed relationships. I had more children this time, as he did. That didn't stop us from getting to know each other.

One day KD asked me about my workout routine. He knew that I was back in the gym and trying to get my body right. He told me about his intense boxing training and asked if I wanted some tips. He asked for my phone number and suggested that we exercise together. I gave him my number and KD immediately sent me a message.

"Are you ready?" KD texted.

I knew his question was two-fold. KD had been trying to get my attention for the longest time. I was curious about this "young bul", which means young guy from Philly. We conversed a lot over the summer of 2013 and became closer. I was going through another difficult transition in my life and needed someone to talk to. I needed someone to be in my corner. KD was very caring and attentive. He listened to me with his ears and his heart. What was growing between KD and me was hard to resist.

One evening, KD invited me to his victory party in Philadelphia. We had been talking for a good while and I had made up my mind that I was, in fact, ready for him. I was living at my parents' house at the time because I was separated from PJB. KD invited his celebrity friends to his celebration too. He had won his prior fight and it seemed like the entire city wanted to party with him. I told him that I would be there and that I would bring my team with me.

My estranged husband, PJB, got wind of the party. He was at rehearsal earlier that day but he rushed to my parents' house to see me. PJB had an idea that I was going to see another man. He asked to go the party with me.

"You can go if you want to," I said to PJB, "but I don't want you there."

"Why don't you want me there?" PJB asked. "What's going on with this dude? Do you love him or somethin'?"

"Yes, I do," I quickly responded.

I couldn't believe that I had admitted the truth to PJB. It felt good to know that I didn't have to hide my feelings anymore. All of the emotions tied to my marriage were gone. Even the anger and the hatred I had felt because of the lying and the infidelity had faded. When I confessed my love for KD, I felt free.

PJB left my parents' house and I headed to Philly to celebrate with my friend. The party was exactly what I needed. I introduced KD to my team and we partied like it was the end of the world. In the middle of the event, I asked KD to walk with me to the bathroom. As always, I never wanted to be alone. KD didn't mind the request. He even went into the bathroom and made sure nothing happened to me. His willingness to protect me was impressive. His sweet nature spoke to me on another level.

KD waited patiently for me in the restroom. When I walked over to wash my hands, KD was standing near the hand dryer. I was very curious about KD and I knew that there was something special between us. I didn't know how deep my feelings were for him but I needed to know. I wanted to kiss him badly. I knew that if I felt something when I kissed him then there would be no turning back. The moment of truth had arrived.

I walked behind KD and he turned around. Our faces

were inches apart and I decided to make my move. I kissed him on the lips. The sensual moment we shared was magical. Our kiss only lasted a few seconds but the feeling has never faded. We looked at each other for a brief moment. Our souls connected.

"Let's get out of here before people start thinking we are in here doing something crazy," KD said.

I agreed and smiled at him. We pulled ourselves together to leave the bathroom. KD stared into my eyes.

"I fuckin' love you," KD said.

"I love you too." I said with a smile.

We left the bathroom feeling like we were on cloud nine. We were at his victory party but I felt like I was celebrating that fact that KD had won my heart. Later that evening, KD walked me to my car. My team was there to witness a new love in my life. They were happy to see me happy again.

KD and I started a relationship a few months later. He stayed patient with me as I filmed another season of RB Divas: LA. When I returned to a disheveled house during my thirty days of hell, KD was there to support me and help put my life back in order.

Our love is something that I have never felt before. KD makes me feel loved and protected. He provides for me like no other. KD makes me feel like I matter. KD makes my children feel like they are his own. I have never felt this loved, this covered, and this beautiful in my life.

For the past thirteen years, I have been singing songs about love and relationships. I wanted to speak my happiness into existence. After my failed relationships, I felt like I was living a lie. I never knew that it would take nearly a decade and a half to find true love. One day, I asked KD to tell me what he wanted from me. Despite our intense love, I was well aware of the challenges on the horizon. KD was honest with me.

"I want you to motivate me," KD told me. "I need you to keep me focused. That's what every man needs. It's crazy out here in this world. I want you to be my last stop. I want you to be my wife."

KD's words touched me deeply. He told me about his failed relationships in the past and agreed that he has never felt a love like ours. What we have is unique. KD is a Muslim man. I am a Christian woman. We don't have Bible battles or religious debates. We never disrespect each other's beliefs. I have prayed with KD and he has visited my Bible study. Despite the naysayers, we make our relationship work. Our love runs deep. Even my father has given us his blessings.

To be embraced by each other's families is something that I have always dreamed of. Ever since I was a young girl, I had searched for the type of love that my parents shared. I believe God has delivered what I needed. Our relationship is not perfect, but the happiness I feel makes my soul smile.

KD reminds me of the story of David in the Bible. David also was a fighter and was wild. He slayed Goliath and defeated many foes. What many forget about David is that he was a man after God's own heart. My connection with KD goes well beyond the physical and emotional. I love his heart and the passion he possesses. For KD to be my last stop would be a dream come true or, as he would say, "Insha'Allah".

*

Cynthia Loving

Epilogue

No one gets to choose his life. I truly believe that God has a destiny planned for all of us. To do the right thing is a personal choice and it is not always easy. As a young woman, I made countless mistakes that could have jeopardized my future. It brings me to tears when I think of how my bad choices could have affected my life and the lives of my children. It's only through the grace of God that I was able to push through the pain and carry on.

A constant battle persists between Cynthia Loving and Lil' Mo. From the day I created the character, I had to fight hard to keep her under control. They say music calms the savage beast. Still, no matter how many hit songs I make, Lil' Mo never seems to calm down. As I move into a new chapter of my life, I realize that a change is needed. When things in my personal life become hectic, I have to remind myself to calm down. When my home life is overwhelming, I have to remember that I have help. When the shady nature of the music industry gets under my skin, I have to resist the urge to fly off the handle and calm down.

Lil' Mo has never been hurt. She was an image I created to help me deal with the issues of my past. Cynthia Loving had to endure the physical and emotional pain of being molested, lied to, cheated on, stolen from, abandoned, and assaulted. I harbored a lot of baggage from those situations. When I decided to forgive the people in my past, my life began to change for the better. I have apologized and mended a lot of relationships that I had damaged over the years. I didn't realize that I was carrying a lot of unnecessary anger with me. It seemed that the character I had created to protect Cynthia Loving was out of control. It is time to tame her. My life has been filled with love since childhood. I always wanted the love that my mom and dad shared. I searched for someone to love and respect me. I poured my heart out unconditionally expecting the same in return. I rushed into relationships and befriended the wrong people. In my search for ultimate happiness, I made some poor choices.

 A comforting peace entered my life when I realized that my journey was never in vain. I had to calm my spirit with the belief that what is meant for me would come to me. For the first time in my life, I don't feel like I have to force things. The happiness I feel is genuine. My happiness had to first come from within if I were going to be a better mother, daughter, friend, wife, and sister. When I was younger, I tried to live a perfect life. In my quest to be the perfect Christian girl, a lot of imperfect things happened to me. After I decided to be happy and at peace with my destiny, countless doors have opened up for my family and me. The glow has returned to my smile. I feel alive again. I'm glad that I didn't stop fighting. I'm happy that I never stopped believing in love and, most importantly, never stopped believing in myself.

I can finally say that I have broken free from my past. The day I decided to let go of all the baggage in my life, everything changed. I released the blame, the bickering, and everything else that I believed was holding me back. The day I decided to be happy was the day that the fight between Cynthia Loving and Lil' Mo was over. I finally have the perfect balance.

We can never plan our lives. We can organize our days but God is in control of our ultimate plan. It took me a long time to realize that my happiness was within. I wasn't always able to recognize the importance of self-love, but God helped me to see my way through. The package was addressed to me my entire life, Cynthia "Lil' Mo" Loving. The love I feel inside is real and I know that all things are possible through Him. God still gets the glory. Pray my skrent.

*

NEXT LEVEL PUBLISHING

ORDER FORM

Name: _____

Address: _____

City / State: _____ **Zip Code:** _____

Email: _____ @ _____

Special Instructions: _____

For Book Signings, Appearances and Lectures
please email taminglilmo@nextlevelpublishing.com

QTY	TITLE	PRICE
	Taming Lil' Mo Paperback ISBN-10: 0980015472 ISBN-13: 978-0980015478	$16.95 usd $19.95 can
	*Shipping & Handling $5.25 /Book	
	TOTAL ORDER	$_____ . __

*Wholesalers, Bookstores, Schools & Institutions please email taminglilmo@nextlevelpublishing.com

Please make all checks and money orders payable to:

Next Level Publishing
c/o Taming Lil' Mo
PO Box 83
Newark, NJ 07101

* Please allow 5-7 Business Days for shipping once payment is received. Please allow 2-3 Weeks for All Institution Orders.

TAMING Lil' Mo

www.TamingLilMo.com

Thank You for Supporting The Literary Arts

NEXT LEVEL PUBLISHING